W9-BXU-446

My Name Is Not Slow

Youth with Mental Retardation

A House Between Homes
Youth in the Foster Care System

A Different Way of Seeing
Youth with Visual Impairments and Blindness

The Ocean Inside
Youth Who Are Deaf and Hard of Hearing

My Name Is Not Slow
Youth with Mental Retardation

Chained
Youth with Chronic Illness

Runaway Train
Youth with Emotional Disturbance

Stuck on Fast Forward
Youth with Attention-Deficit/Hyperactivity Disorder

Why Can't I Learn Like Everyone Else?
Youth with Learning Disabilities

Finding My Voice
Youth with Speech Impairment

Somebody Hear Me Crying
Youth in Protective Services

Guaranteed Rights
The Legislation That Protects Youth with Special Needs

The Journey Toward Recovery
Youth with Brain Injury

Breaking Down Barriers
Youth with Physical Challenges

On the Edge of Disaster
Youth in the Juvenile Court System

The Hidden Child
Youth with Autism

My Name Is Not Slow

Youth with Mental Retardation

BY AUTUMN LIBAL

MASON CREST PUBLISHERS

Mason Crest Publishers Inc.
370 Reed Road
Broomall, Pennsylvania 19008
(866) MCP-BOOK (toll free)

First printing
1 2 3 4 5 6 7 8 9 10

Libal, Autumn.
My name is not Slow: youth with mental retardation / by Autumn Libal.
p. cm.—(Youth with special needs)
Summary: Tells the story of Penelope, a girl who has Down syndrome, her growth and development, and how she and her family are affected by her condition. Includes bibliographical references and index.
1. Children with mental disabilities—Juvenile literature. [1. Down syndrome. 2. People with mental disabilities.] I. Title. II. Series.
HQ773.7.L53 2004
362.3'0835—dc22   2003018435

ISBN 1-59084-731-8
1-59084-727-X (series)

Design by Harding House Publishing Service.
Composition by Bytheway Publishing Services, Inc., Binghamton, New York.
Cover art by Keith Rosko.
Cover design by Benjamin Stewart.
Produced by Harding House Publishing Service, Vestal, New York.
Printed and bound in the Hashemite Kingdom of Jordan.

Picture credits: Benjamin Stewart: pp. 21, 32, 34, 55, 72, 93, 95, 96. Comstock: p. 19. Corbis: p. 42. Corel: pp. 44, 46. Image Source: p. 20. Life Art: pp. 27, 28, 29, 33. Patricia Therrien: p. 92. Photo Alto: pp. 57, 59, 60, 62, 70, 94, 98. PhotoDisc: pp. 22, 23, 24, 81, 90, 91, 107, 109, 110. Photospin: pp. 82, 108. Research Foundation/Camp Abilities: pp. 25, 31, 71, 78, 97, 118, 119. The individuals in the Comstock, Corbis, Photo Alto, PhotoDisc, and Photospin images are models, and the images are for illustrative purposes only.

CONTENTS

A child with special needs is not defined by his disability.
It is just one part of who he is.

INTRODUCTION

Each child is unique and wonderful. And some children have differences we call special needs. Special needs can mean many things. Sometimes children will learn differently, or hear with an aid, or read with Braille. A young person may have a hard time communicating or paying attention. A child can be born with a special need, or acquire it by an accident or through a health condition. Sometimes a child will be developing in a typical manner and then become delayed in that development. But whatever problems a child may have with her learning, emotions, behavior, or physical body, she is always a person first. She is not defined by her disability; instead, the disability is just one part of who she is.

Inclusion means that young people with and without special needs are together in the same settings. They learn together in school; they play together in their communities; they all have the same opportunities to belong. Children learn so much from each other. A child with a hearing impairment, for example, can teach another child a new way to communicate using sign language. Someone else who has a physical disability affecting his legs can show his friends how to play wheelchair basketball. Children with and without special needs can teach each other how to appreciate and celebrate their differences. They can also help each other discover how people are more alike than they are different. Understanding and appreciating how we all have similar needs helps us learn empathy and sensitivity.

In this series, you will read about young people with special needs from the unique perspectives of children and adolescents who are experiencing the disability firsthand. Of course, not all children with a particular disability are the same as the characters in the stories. But the stories demonstrate at an emotional level how a special need impacts a child, his family, and his friends. The factual material in each chapter will expand your horizons by adding to your knowledge about a particular disability. The series as a whole will help you understand differences better and appreciate how they make us all stronger and better.

—Cindy Croft
Educational Consultant

YOUTH WITH SPECIAL NEEDS provides a unique forum for demystifying a wide variety of childhood medical and developmental disabilities. Written to captivate an adolescent audience, the books bring to life the challenges and triumphs experienced by children with common chronic conditions such as hearing loss, mental retardation, physical differences, and speech difficulties. The topics are addressed frankly through a blend of fiction and fact. Students and teachers alike can move beyond the information provided by accessing the resources offered at the end of each text.

This series is particularly important today as the number of children with special needs is on the rise. Over the last two decades, advances in pediatric medical techniques have allowed children who have chronic illnesses and disabilities to live longer, more functional lives. As a result, these children represent an increasingly visible part of North American population in all aspects of daily life. Students are exposed to peers with special needs in their classrooms, through extracurricular activities, and in the community. Often, young people have misperceptions and unanswered questions about a child's disabilities—and more important, his or her *abilities*. Many times, there is no vehicle for talking about these complex issues in a comfortable manner.

This series provides basic information that will leave readers with a deeper understanding of each condition, along with an awareness of some of the associated emotional impacts on affected children, their families, and their peers. It will also encourage further conversation about these issues. Most important, the series promotes a greater comfort for its readers as they live, play, and work side by side with these individuals who have medical and developmental differences—youth with special needs.

—*Dr. Lisa Albers, Dr. Carolyn Bridgemohan, Dr. Laurie Glader*
Medical Consultants

Every child—even those whom adults believe are broken
or imperfect—carry a message of hope to our world.
—Annmarie Joseph

1

THE BIGGEST DECISION OF THEIR LIVES

When Mrs. Brown learned she was pregnant again, her first feeling was fear. Pregnancy and childbirth had been hard enough when she was in her twenties. She could not imagine what it was going to be like now that she was forty-six years old. Mr. Brown was fearful, too. He was frightened for his wife and her health, but he was frightened for himself as well. Even if all went well with the pregnancy and birth, many more struggles would follow. He and his wife weren't young anymore, and he knew that the diapers, doctor appointments, sleepless nights, and endless demands of yet another baby would not be easy.

Then there were other things to consider. Soon big college bills would be rolling in and wouldn't stop for twelve years—the amount of time it would take for their three existing children to graduate. How were they going to pay for a baby and college at the same time? Worse yet, when their new baby was finally ready to go off to college as well, Mr. and Mrs. Brown would be sixty-four years old—an age they had hoped to spend in carefree retirement.

So Mr. Brown held his breath. Mrs. Brown cried some sleepless nights. And they both wondered what they were going to say to their children.

Krista, Phillip, and Jonathan had been totally unprepared for the news. Family conferences were a rare thing in their home. So when they were called to the kitchen table for "a talk," the children's hearts thumped with apprehension as they contemplated which laws they had broken.

As she made her way toward the kitchen, eighteen-year-old Krista thought about the college acceptance letter she had stuffed deep in the garbage. It was from Kansas State University, the college in her hometown. That's where her parents wanted her to go—to save money they said. Krista was sure their real reason was to keep her close to home. She had her heart set on Berkeley—the West Coast, beach-bound California. Heading for the kitchen table, Krista drew her shoulders back and strengthened her resolve. It did not matter if they found the letter, she told herself. She was not going to Kansas State.

While Krista strategized for the expected fight, fifteen-year-old Phillip approached the family conference contemplating his own fate. The past few weekends he'd told his parents he was going to the movies with his friends, but he spent the evenings making out in his girlfriend's car instead. Everyone thought he was the luckiest guy in school because his girlfriend was sixteen and could drive. He wouldn't feel lucky for long, however, if his parents found out what he was actually doing on Saturday nights.

Fear and guilt twisted in twelve-year-old Jonathan's chest as well. Last night, two of his friends had come over to play video games in the basement. Taking the beer had been his friends' idea, but Jonathan had gone along with it. He thought they should only take one and split it, but his friends told him to stop being a baby and take three, one for each of them. Three missing beers would be a lot easier for his parents to notice than one, but what was he going to say to his friends? So he snuck the three cans from the fridge and concealed his grimace as he slugged down the awful-tasting liquid. Later, Jonathan stowed the empty cans in the recycling bin. Looking at his parents' drawn faces, he thought maybe the extra cans had been detected after all. *Blame it on Phillip*, he told himself as he dragged his feet toward the table, *on Phillip first and then on Krista*.

The chairs squeaked across the linoleum floor as Mr. and Mrs.

Brown sat down to face their children. They did not even notice the way their children squirmed, for truthfully, Mr. and Mrs. Brown were squirming inwardly as well.

Jonathan's first reaction to his mother's news that she was pregnant was relief. *At least they haven't discovered the beer cans,* he thought with a sigh. After his initial relief passed, however, he contemplated his parents' news. Why was everyone looking so serious? A new baby didn't seem like that big of deal. In fact, it sounded like a pretty good thing. Jonathan had always been the baby of the family. Having a little brother or sister would be cool. Jonathan would be the big brother for once. The more he thought about it, the more he liked the idea.

While Jonathan was thinking about becoming a big brother, his parents were talking about money and sacrifices. Phillip wasn't sure he liked the sound of that. "What kind of sacrifices?" Phillip wondered aloud.

"Well, for instance," his father replied slowly, "the baby is going to need a bedroom. You and Jonathan might have to share a room for a while." Phillip looked aghast at the possibility, but it was Krista who appeared most alarmed.

"Why can't the baby have my room?" she questioned, suspicion sharpening her voice. "I'll be at college." She knew something else was coming—something she wouldn't like. Mr. and Mrs. Brown looked at one another.

"Well, that's another thing we're going to have to discuss." Mrs. Brown spoke in slow, careful words, and Krista held her breath. "We know you've had your heart set on going to college in California, but you have to understand that with a new baby, we just won't be able to afford it."

Krista's heart sank. It was a plot! All a plot to keep her home!

"We know it's not what you had hoped for," Krista's father put in. "But your mother and I think the best thing is for you to go to Kansas State and live here to save some money."

Krista's face twisted. "I can't believe you expect me to throw away all my dreams just because you two were stupid enough to go and get pregnant again!" Krista's chair clattered on the floor as she stood and gripped the table with white-knuckled hands. "You're ruining my life! I hate you!" She spun away from her parents and stomped from the room, leaving the kitchen door swinging behind her.

Mr. Brown sighed while Mrs. Brown's face puckered as though she were holding back tears.

"Jonathan and I can share a room," Phillip offered quietly, but his mother just buried her face in her hands.

The months that passed were a mix of tension, excitement, and apprehension in the Brown household. As compensation for making them share a bedroom, Mr. and Mrs. Brown told Phillip and Jonathan they could decorate the room any way they wanted. To Mrs. Brown's dismay, the boys decided to paint their bedroom black and hang a camouflage curtain down the middle, separating their two sides. They were also hoping for a television in their shared room. Their parents hadn't given in yet, but Phillip and Jonathan were pretty sure that with so many other things going on they could wear down their parents.

If the prospect of a new baby was bringing the brothers closer together, it was tearing Krista from the rest of the family. Krista barely spoke to her father and refused to acknowledge her mother. She stalked around the house with a permanent scowl and performed her household chores with violent, jerking motions, as if every movement was a protest against her unfair life. At times, Phillip considered informing his sister about how selfish she was being, but her stomping and fuming intimidated him, so like everyone else, he met her displeasure with silence.

And so life in the Brown household continued until the family received a devastating piece of news.

Mr. and Mrs. Brown sat down in the doctor's office to learn the results of the ***amniocentesis***. In a few moments, they would know whether they were having a boy or a girl. For the first time in months, Mrs. Brown felt excited. When she had first learned that she was pregnant, a dark veil of depression had fallen over her. She had not been pleased at the prospect of starting parenthood all over again. But the passing months had given her time to think. She felt the new child growing and moving inside her, and the veil of sadness began to give way to a new joy.

"Mrs. Brown," the doctor said, "it's a girl." Mrs. Brown's heart doubled its pace at his words—two girls and two boys, a perfect family. But the doctor's pronouncements had not stopped there. "Unfortunately, I have to give you some very difficult news," the doctor said. "The genetic tests reveal that your baby will be born with Down syndrome."

She felt her husband squeezing her hand, but Mrs. Brown stared blankly ahead. *What did he say?* she wondered, his words processing too slowly in her brain. Down syndrome? Her baby with Down syndrome? Her newfound joy deflated like a ball that bounced empty and lifeless in the hollow cavity of her chest. She felt the veil of sorrow descending once again.

For the remainder of the visit, only snippets of the doctor's words came to Mrs. Brown's ears: "Heart condition . . . impaired sight . . . physical abnormalities." Each statement stung. But of all the hopeless-sounding phrases the doctor spoke, two words burned worse than all the rest: "Mental retardation."

By the time the appointment was over, Mrs. Brown had already made up her mind. The diagnosis of Down syndrome was a sign. This child was not meant to be a part of their family. Nothing in their lives had made sense since finding out she was pregnant. Raising a baby would be difficult enough. Raising a baby with mental retardation seemed impossible. There was only one answer. She would not have this baby. Driving home in the car, Mr. Brown agreed.

Mrs. Brown scheduled the appointment for the abortion. It would have to be done fast. The more time that passed, the larger the *fetus* grew, and the more dangerous the procedure would be. The mood in the house was somber. In three days, their lives would be back to normal, but no one seemed relieved.

The night before the abortion, Krista joined her mother on the porch. They had barely spoken for months, and the silence of those days weighed heavily on Krista's heart. She wished she hadn't spent so much time being angry. It would be easier to tell her mother the news if Krista hadn't built such a wall between them.

"I didn't get into Berkeley, Mom," Krista began in hesitant tones. "I didn't want to tell you guys because I'd made such a big fuss about not wanting to go to Kansas State, but I guess I'll be going there after all." Krista fought hot tears as she spoke, hoping her mother would forgive her.

Krista watched her mother struggling silently. These past few days had made her look tired and old. When she finally spoke, it was in slow, remorseful tones. "I'm so sorry, Krista. I know that none of this is what you wanted. It's not what any of us wanted." She paused and the silence hung between them.

"Mom, I'm sorry about the way I've acted." It was all Krista could think to say. Her mother nodded, took a deep breath, and laid her head back against her chair. She raised her hand to her distended stomach.

"I can feel the baby moving," was her quiet reply. They sat like this for a moment, each cradling her own private pain, until Krista built the courage to bridge the silence again.

"I've been thinking these past few days about how everybody wants a perfect baby." Krista spoke the words quietly, unable to look at her mother as she spoke. "And we all think we know what perfect is." She paused for a moment afraid to continue, then blurted out her thought all at once. "But who's to say that a baby with Down syndrome isn't God's idea of a perfect baby?"

Mother and daughter sat in silence. Krista was afraid she might have said the wrong thing, but after a moment her mother smiled. It was the first genuine smile she had seen on her mother's face in months.

"Do you want to feel the baby moving?" Mrs. Brown asked her daughter. Krista nodded her head solemnly. Mrs. Brown gently took her daughter's hand and guided it to her swollen belly. "Can you feel that?" she asked with a smile.

Krista studied her mother's face. It was still too soon for her to feel the tiny baby's movements through her mother's stomach, but she nodded her head anyway. "Yes, I can feel her moving."

Tears ran down the women's faces as they clasped each other's hands. Krista laid her face on her mother's stomach, and Mrs. Brown wove her fingers gently through her daughter's hair. "It's okay, Krista. Everything's going to be okay."

The next day, Mrs. Brown canceled her appointment with the clinic.

THE CHOICES PARENTS FACE

Mr. and Mrs. Brown are facing an unexpected event in their lives—having another child when they thought their child-raising years were coming to a close. The prospect of having a baby can cause many different emotions. Some people will be thrilled to be having a child while other people may be sad. Some people may feel that they are at the perfect point in their lives for raising children. At other times, however, people may not have the money or *familial* support to raise a child properly. Perhaps they feel they are too young or too old to take on the responsibility of caring for another human being. Whatever the circumstances, having a child always involves life changes and requires careful consideration and planning.

When families learn they are having another child, they need to make many difficult decisions. They need to decide how the child will fit into their existing family and how they will financially support the child. However, when medical tests show that the baby will be born with a medical condition, decisions become even more difficult—and they may be asked decide whether they will have the baby at all.

In some cases, information about a baby's medical condition can be learned from a test called amniocentesis. In this procedure, a needle is inserted through a pregnant woman's abdomen and into her uterus to take a sample of the amniotic fluid that surrounds and protects the growing baby. As the baby grows, some of its skin cells fall off and float in the amniotic fluid. When a sample of this fluid is taken, doctors can look at the *DNA* in the floating skin cells and determine whether the baby will have certain *genetic* disorders. Sometimes, if these tests detect a genetic disorder, the parents will decide not to have the baby.

When a women first learns that her child will have Down syndrome, a genetic disorder that causes mental retardation

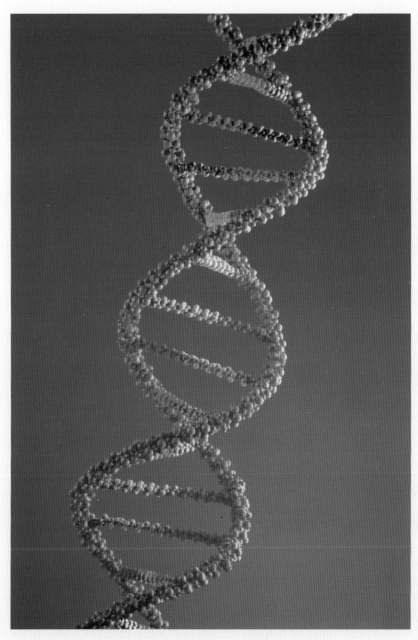

A model representing a strand of DNA.

(among other things), she may decide not to have the child. Her feelings of uncertainty are perfectly normal. Most parents upon learning that their child will have a condition like mental retardation feel fear and disappointment, which may cause them to question the wisdom of bringing the child into the world. These feelings are not simply selfish. Most often the parents are concerned, not only about how the child will affect their own lives but about the type of life their child will have. They fear that living with mental retardation will be painful for their child, causing her to have an unhappy life. They question the fairness of bringing a child into the world who will always have to struggle with disabilities and other people's prejudices. There are no easy answers to questions like these. Many parents struggle with their initial emotions and decide to have their child.

Many forms of mental retardation are caused at the genetic level.

Students who are mentally retarded may go to special schools designed to meet their needs.

WHAT IS MENTAL RETARDATION?

The American Psychiatric Association's *Diagnostic and Statistical Manual,* fourth edition, lists three criteria for a diagnosis of mental retardation:

1. significantly subaverage intellectual functioning
2. significant limitations in at least two of the following skills:
   - communication
   - self-care
   - home living
   - social/interpersonal skills
   - use of community resources
   - self-direction
   - functional academic skills
   - work
   - leisure
   - health
   - safety
3. onset before age 18 years

The mind of a person with mental retardation will work more slowly.

Mental retardation is a medical term given to any condition that causes a person's mind to develop and work more slowly than the average person's mind does. Approximately sixty million people around the world have mental retardation. About 7.2 million of those people live in the United States.

One of the ways that people test to see if a person has mental retardation is with an intelligence **quotient** test (an IQ test). Most people usually score between 81 and 109 on IQ tests. If a child routinely scores below seventy on this test, she may have mental retardation. Some people feel that IQ tests are not accurate ways of measuring intelligence, but for now it is still the test that most medical professionals and educators use. IQ tests mainly measure a child's potential ability to perform in school, rather than the ability to perform life functions; as a result, IQ should be recognized as an artificial concept, rather than an absolute measurement of some concrete, measurable quality. Social and cultural background and native language influence IQ scores, as do sensory, physical movement, and communication disabilities.

Other characteristics a psychologist, medical professional, or educator will look for are whether or not the child has limitations in two or more adaptive skill areas (like listening, speaking, moving, reading, and others), and that these limitations began before the child turned eighteen.

The term mental retardation, though used extensively in the medical field, is very hurtful to many people. In our society, people with mental retardation are highly **stigmatized** and face **discrimination** and ridicule. Many people feel that the term mental retardation invites judgment and

NURSES ONLY

Individuals with mental retardation may need special care and supervision.

scorn and would prefer that terms like **cognitive** delays, special needs, mental handicaps, intellectual disabilities, learning disabilities, and **developmental** delays be used instead. Many organizations that help people with mental retardation have adopted other terms to refer to these conditions. However, mental retardation is still the term most often used by the medical, mental health, and educational fields and is used in this book because most people are more familiar with this term and therefore understand it better than some of the other terms.

WHAT CAUSES MENTAL RETARDATION?

Many different things can cause intellectual delays, but according to something called the Two-Group Theory, there are two major categories of mental retardation: organic and cultural-familial.

The Organic Group

This category consists of all forms of mental retardation that have a known genetic or physical cause. For example, someone born with mental retardation due to a genetic condition such as Down syndrome would have an organic reason for their symptoms of mental retardation. Additionally, anyone who has mental retardation caused by physical damage to the brain (such as from a serious head injury or a very bad illness prior to 18 years of age) also falls into the organic category. People with organic reasons for mental retardation often have serious intellectual disabilities combined with physical disabilities. Organic forms of mental retardation happen to people in all groups and levels of society, regardless of race, culture, economic status, or education.

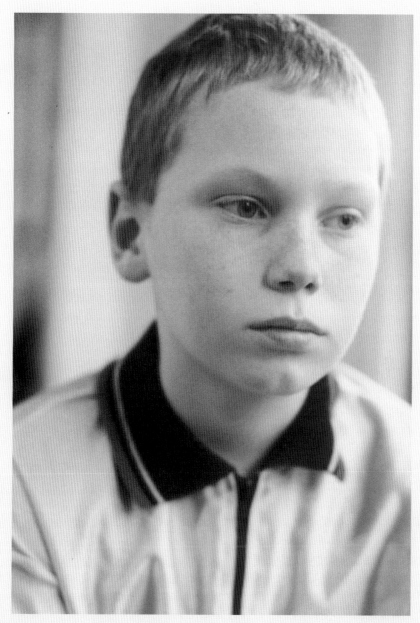

The term "mental retardation" can be hurtful. Individuals are always more than any label.

All of these are possible causes of mental retardation:

- inherited (genetic) disorders or *chromosome* defects
- abuse of certain drugs or alcohol during pregnancy
- specific infections during pregnancy
- malnutrition before and after birth (essential periods of brain development)
- complications of prematurity
- severe bleeding at birth
- birth injury or lack of oxygen during delivery
- glandular problems (for example, **hypothyroidism**)
- toxins that affect the brain (for example, lead poisoning)
- accidents that cause brain damage

Since so many of these causes have their roots in pregnancy and delivery, adequate medical care and nutrition are essential throughout all pregnancies.

Environmental Factors

This category consists of people who have mental retardation but have no identifiable organic cause for their condition. People in this group generally have much milder forms of mental retardation than people in the organic group have, and they do not have any accompanying physical disabilities. This form of mental retardation is thought to be caused by different environmental factors affecting a young child. For example, the first three years of a child's life are the most important years for language and other forms of development. Proper nutrition, physical affection, and intellectual stimulation are extremely important and will affect the child's potential to learn and develop for the rest of her life. Studies have shown that children who are severely physically, emotionally, and intellectually neglected in these early

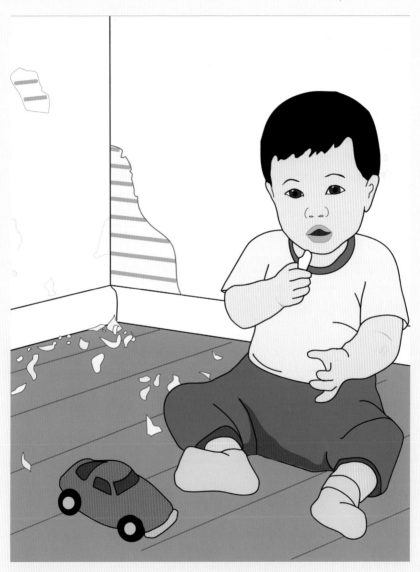

Lead poisoning from old paint is one cause of mental retardation.

years (for example, if a child is locked in a room and not given any contact with other people) may never fully recover and may even develop mild mental retardation. Such a form of mental retardation, for which there is a social or environmental rather than an organic cause, would be categorized as part of the cultural-familial group.

WHAT IS DOWN SYNDROME?

Down syndrome is only one of many different conditions that is associated with mental retardation. It is a genetic condition caused by having an extra twenty-first chromosome in each cell. Chromosomes in each of your cells are where all of the

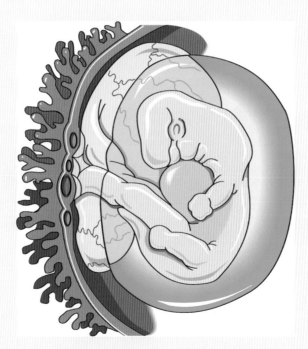

Many causes of mental retardation begin at the very earliest stages of life.

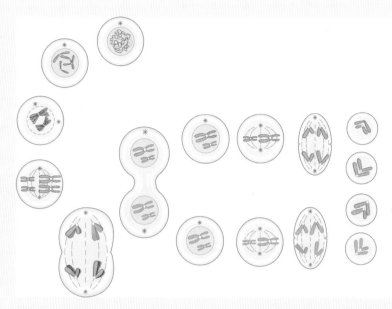

When cells divide to form a new life, things do not always work out as expected.

genetic information that determines how you will develop is stored. Most people have forty-six chromosomes, twenty-three from their mother and twenty-three from their father. When a father's sperm joins with a mother's egg, the forty-six chromosomes unite, forming twenty-three pairs with two chromosomes in each pair. The fertilized egg now has all the genetic information it needs to form into a new, unique child.

The joining of the sperm and egg may sound like a simple process, but it is complex. Not everything always works out as it is expected. Sometimes the chromosomes do not join or separate as they are supposed to. Sometimes there are three chromosomes in the twenty-first pair instead of two. When this happens, the child that forms will have Down syndrome. In other cases, a piece of the twenty-first chromosome might break off and join to a different set of chromosomes. This will also cause the new child to form with Down syndrome.

A child with Down syndrome typically develops with some of the following characteristics and conditions:

- upward-slanting eyes with narrow eye slits
- a flat-seeming face with a low-bridged nose
- low-set ears
- broad feet with short toes and broad hands with short fingers
- one crease across the palm of the hand
- arms and legs that are short and a head that is small in comparison to the rest of the body
- large tongue or small mouth that makes the tongue seem large and stick out
- poor muscle tone
- vision problems
- heart conditions
- **thyroid** problems
- bone and joint problems
- **epilepsy**
- ear, nose, and throat problems
- developmental delays (mental retardation in older children)

A person with Down syndrome may be born with only a few or with many of these conditions. The child's conditions may be mild and relatively easy to cope with or they may be severe enough to threaten or shorten the child's life.

A woman's chances of giving birth to a baby with Down syndrome increase as she gets older. Before the age of thirty-five, a woman has about a one in eight hundred to one thousand chance of giving birth to a child with Down syndrome. After the age of thirty-five, she has approximately a one in four hundred chance of having a baby with Down syndrome. After the age of forty, however, her chances

A person with Down syndrome enjoys getting together with friends at a neighborhood park.

Each person has unique gifts all her own. People who are mentally retarded often enjoy music.

increase to about one in 110. Once she is over the age of forty-five, her chances rise to one in thirty-five.

People once thought that individuals with conditions that cause mental retardation had nothing to offer to society. Today, however, most people better understand conditions like Down syndrome. Every person has special gifts, abilities, and talents. A person with Down syndrome may not look like everybody else and may not be able to do all the same things that other people can do, but will still have her own unique abilities. People with Down syndrome may need extra support from their families and communities; nevertheless, they can live full, happy, and productive lives.

OTHER GENETIC SYNDROMES THAT ARE ASSOCIATED WITH MENTAL RETARDATION

Fragile-X Syndrome

This is the second most common genetic cause of mental retardation. According to the American Psychiatric Press's *Textbook of Psychiatry*, it occurs in one out of every thousand males. At least one of the X chromosomes of individuals with this syndrome will appear to be weak or fragile looking. Because girls are usually protected by having two X chromosomes (while boys have an X and a Y), this syndrome is much more common in males. Individuals with this syndrome range from having normal intelligence to having mild to severe retardation, with abnormal facial features that include large jaws, foreheads, and ears.

Normal Female Karyotype

Normal Male Karyotype

Cri du Chat Syndrome

This syndrome is much more rare, occurring in only one out of every 20,000 live births. Children with this syndrome make a distinctive noise that sounds like a cat's cry, and they are usually severely retarded. They are small and grow slowly, with small, round heads and faces that lack **symmetry**. Their eyes are wide set, with skin folds on the inner lids. Children with Cri du Chat usually learn to walk, but their language development is generally an area of difficulty for them throughout their lives.

Trisomy 18 and Trisomy 13

Children with these syndromes have extra eighteenth or thirteenth chromosomes in each of their cells. Again, these

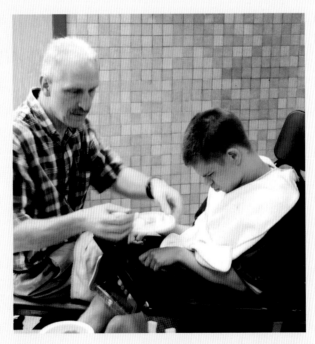

People who are more seriously retarded may need help eating.

disorders are very rare. The children born with either of these disorders will be profoundly retarded, and most do not live past their first year because of related medical problems, including congenital heart disease, **apnea**, or seizures.

INTRAUTERINE CAUSES OF MENTAL RETARDATION

These are causes of mental retardation that occur during pregnancy, when the child is still in the mother's uterus. The three most common are:

1. Fetal Alcohol syndrome. This occurs when the mother exposes her unborn child to high levels of alcohol. It is associated with mild mental retardation. Children with this syndrome tend to be small, with flat cheeks, a flat area between their upper lip and their nose, and thin upper lip.
2. asphyxia. This occurs when the baby does not get enough oxygen before or during birth. It can be caused by the mother's **hypertension**, **toxemia**, or **placenta previa**.
3. infections. Two of the most common are rubella (or German measles) and toxoplasmosis, a disease often caught from cats.

Although individuals with each of these disorders share many things in common, they are—like all of us—individuals. Each person will have a range of abilities with a unique personality all his own.

It takes a family to raise a child.
—Robert Dole

2

SMILE FOR ME, PENELOPE

Everything was quiet the day Penelope Brown was born. As Mrs. Brown's pregnancy grew, she got the sense that the whole world was holding its breath, waiting for a release.

And then one morning, it was time for her daughter to be born. When the doctor finally lifted the baby out of her stomach, Mrs. Brown could not hear her daughter crying. She only caught the briefest glimpse of a limp, bluish arm and a tiny, rolling head as the doctors whisked her daughter from the room.

As another doctor sewed the deep incision in her abdomen back together, Mrs. Brown felt a powerful urge to sleep. She fought to keep her eyes open, to listen to her husband's voice, to discover where they had taken her daughter, but exhaustion threatened to overwhelm her. Then yet another doctor entered the room. "There's a defect in your baby's heart," he explained. "It can be corrected with surgery," Mrs. Brown heard him say, ". . . being prepped for surgery as we speak," but she felt as though she were in a fog. Then Mrs. Brown fell asleep.

Mr. Brown peered through the glass window at his tiny daughter so newly out of surgery. She looked impossibly frail in the ***incubator***, surrounded by beeping, metallic machines. Since his wife had decided not to have an abortion, a war had raged in Mr. Brown's heart. He had never thought they would conceive a child and not bring that child into the world. But then he looked at his other children, Krista brilliant at her schoolwork, Phillip an expert

37

swimmer, Jonathan who loved to paint and sing, and questioned the wisdom of his wife's decision. What kind of a life would their new child have? What would she be able to do? Would she ever have talents like his other children? Would she feel joy from her accomplishments or only pain from her limitations?

But now, standing alone under the florescent lights of the hospital hallway, a wall of glass dividing him from his tiny newborn, Mr. Brown felt a surge of love and desperation. "Beat little heart," he whispered quietly to the motionless body. "Don't give up." He suddenly wished he could apologize to the helpless little being for all of his months of doubt and turmoil, but all Mr. Brown could do was plead, "Please, don't give up now."

The next day, Krista, Phillip, and Jonathan went to the hospital to see their new sister. Mr. Brown warned the children that Penelope was very delicate, since she had just undergone serious surgery, and she might not look the way they expected. Their father's warnings just made the children feel more nervous as they approached the window.

As Krista gazed across the intensive care unit, she felt a mixture of alarm and awe. "How is she ever going to survive?" Krista wondered aloud, feeling both amazed and fearful for the little life.

Jonathan felt confused and disappointed by what he saw. There were so many tubes and instruments attached to the little body that he could barely see his sister at all. *She almost doesn't even look human,* he thought. *With all those tubes, it's like she's an alien or something.* As if she had read his mind, Mrs. Brown reached up from her wheelchair and patted her youngest son on the back.

"It's okay, Jonathan," she comforted. "She'll look different when we bring her home."

"Do all those things hurt?" Jonathan asked.

Mrs. Brown hesitated. She wanted to say they did not, but honestly she did not know. "I hope not, Jonathan," was all she could say.

Of all the family members gathered outside the intensive care unit, Phillip was the only one who felt calm. He didn't know why, but somehow he just knew that his little sister was going to be okay.

He watched her wrinkly feet move slightly, giving barely visible kicks, and he thought that she seemed like a swimmer underwater. She might appear lost in a murky world right now, but Phillip knew that deep down his sister was kicking and fighting. Before they knew it, Phillip was sure Penelope was going to break the surface and take her first big, gasping breath of life.

In a few more days, Penelope did just that. The day Mrs. Brown was able to hold her daughter for the first time everything seemed to change. Resting in her mother's arms, Penelope seemed to breathe easier, to eat better, and to sleep sounder. Soon, she was strong enough to be moved out of the intensive care unit and into her mother's hospital room. The doctors were amazed by how quickly her condition improved. A month after she was born, Penelope was able to go home to start her new life with her family.

Penelope had very little muscle tone when she was born. She did not lift and wave her limbs as other babies do. Her head lolled about on her shoulders, as floppy as if it were disconnected. Her floppiness made Krista nervous. Most of the time, Krista was afraid to hold Penelope; she had the feeling Penelope could suddenly break. So Krista avoided physical contact with her little sister and tried to make herself useful in other ways—by warming up bottles, making dinners for the family, and picking up groceries on the way home from school—all things that were helpful, but that didn't involve touching her fragile sister too much.

Having had three babies already, Mr. and Mrs. Brown were not frightened of their daughter, but they were exhausted. As they spent hours rocking and feeding the tiny baby, days constantly changing diapers, and weeks running to doctor's appointments, they found themselves wishing that they were twenty years younger.

More than anything else, Jonathan was bored with his little sister. Before Penelope came home from the hospital, Jonathan made a mobile of colorful, dancing animals to hang from her crib. He had been very excited about becoming a big brother and doing things with his little sister. But Penelope hardly did anything at all. All she seemed to do was sleep. She hadn't even noticed the mobile swinging above her. In the beginning, Jonathan had often tried to gain Penelope's attention by bouncing the animals on their mobile strings or dancing around to catch Penelope's gaze, but she barely seemed to look at him at all. She did not babble or laugh or even smile. As the months went by, Jonathan began thinking sadly of his sister as nothing more than a little eating, sleeping, mess-making machine.

A little older than Jonathan and understanding Penelope's medical condition better, Phillip was not discouraged. He knew that one of these days, Penelope was going to look about and begin taking notice of the world around her. Nearly every day after school, Phillip told Penelope about his day. Sometimes, if his parents were in another room, he leaned over the side of Penelope's crib and whispered to her about his girlfriend—telling Penelope secrets about things his girlfriend had said and places that they went, secrets he knew Penelope would keep. Other days, he told Penelope about his swim meets. He described the races that he swam. Sometimes he even acted them out, reliving the laps, and ending by telling Penelope that when she was bigger, he'd teach her how to swim.

A whole year wore on. Penelope rarely seemed to notice what Phillip was doing. Sometimes she didn't even look at him as he spoke, but that didn't stop him from giving his performances and talking to her, because he knew that somewhere inside, she was listening.

It was during one of these performances, as Phillip's arms were swinging and his mouth gasping in a reenactment of the final lap of a race, that an amazing thing happened. Mrs. Brown was bouncing Penelope on her lap as Phillip breast stroked through the air toward her. Phillip lifted his head for a breath, and was just about to dive back into the imaginary water, when he froze. A grin spread across his face, and he pointed at Penelope.

"Look, Mom," he whispered, trying to contain his excitement, afraid the moment would break. "Look, Penelope is smiling. She's smiling for me."

HIGH-RISK BIRTH

Women give birth to babies all the time, and normally everything goes just fine. However, the regular birth process can
be difficult, not only for the mother, but for the baby as well.
There is potential for some things to go wrong. As a baby
passes through the narrow birth canal, his head and body
are squeezed. If the baby is very delicate or has a serious
medical condition, he could be harmed during birth. If the
placenta, the organ that carries nutrient- and oxygen-rich
blood to the baby, detaches from the uterine wall too soon,
the baby might begin to suffocate.

When doctors already know that a baby will be born
with a serious medical condition, or if the mother is older, a
woman's pregnancy would be called a high-risk pregnancy.
In a high-risk pregnancy, a doctor may perform a cesarean
section. This procedure involves removing the baby through
a cut in the mother's abdomen. A cesarean section mini-
mizes the risk of harm to the mother or baby during the
birth process.

GOING HOME

In the past, many children with mental retardation were sent
to live in institutions or mental hospitals. Parents who had
children with mental retardation or other special needs were
encouraged to give away their children. Often, these children were raised without the physical, emotional, and intellectual care and stimulation they needed. Many children
sent to live in institutions were never able to reach their full
potential, not because they weren't capable of growth and
accomplishment, but because no one valued them or cared
enough to help them. Think how hard it would be for you
to learn and grow if no one ever taught you, showed you
love, or encouraged you.

Today, most people understand that the best thing for almost any child, including children with mental retardation or other special needs, is to be raised by his own family in his own home.

WHO'S AFRAID OF THE BIG, BAD . . . BABY?

It is quite common for new parents to be frightened when they have their first child. It is even more common for people to be frightened when a new baby has a medical condition like Down syndrome. Parents and siblings may think the baby looks delicate and frail. This may make them afraid that they will hurt the baby if they touch him.

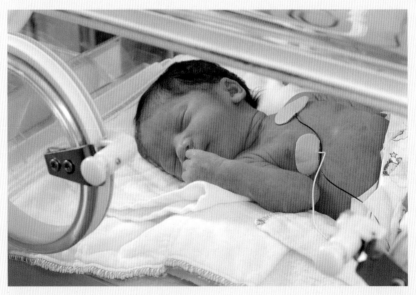

Premature babies are more apt to have medical conditions that can cause mental retardation.

But all babies need love and attention. Physical contact is one of the most important ways that humans show their love. Physical contact is especially important to babies because they cannot yet understand spoken language. Every child needs closeness and attention.

Underdeveloped muscles leave an infant's limbs and head limp, a common feature of conditions like Down syndrome—but the infant will not break if she is held. In fact, it is more harmful to avoid giving a child physical attention than risking picking up the delicate child. Furthermore, because a child with mental retardation will be slower to learn language than other children, it is even more important that parents and family members show the child their love with physical affection.

HOW IMPORTANT IS A SMILE?

Most of us take smiles for granted. After all, smiling is something that everyone does. We usually do it many times a day. But we are not born knowing how to smile. It is something that we learn. A baby's first smile is an important developmental accomplishment.

Babies are usually very curious and interested in their world. Before they can talk, laugh, or even smile, they observe the world around them with wide, watchful eyes. They may not look like they are doing much, but they are learning at a faster rate than they will learn at any other point in their lives.

Despite how common mental retardation is, misconceptions about mental retardation are common. Many people think that people with mental retardation are "funny-looking" or "weird." Mentally retarded adults are often treated as though they are still children.

People with mental retardation are human beings just like everyone else. A young child diagnosed with symptoms of

Learning to smile is an important milestone in a baby's development.

mental retardation will not always be a child; he will continue to learn, change, and grow intellectually, like any other child, but at a much slower rate than his same-age peers.

Children with mental retardation may begin speaking later than other children and may have trouble learning certain things. Many children with mental retardation will have delayed physical development as well. For example, they may start sitting, crawling, and walking later than the average child, or they may have difficulty with balance and coordination.

This table shows the average ages for 50–95 percent of all children for behaviors that are considered developmental milestones:

Age	Behavior
3–6 months	uses whole hand to grasp
1–3 months	smiles
3–6 months	sits up
6–8 months	crawls
8 months	exhibits stranger anxiety
9 months	exhibits separation anxiety
10–16 months	walks alone
15 months	imitates vocal sounds
18 months	talks (uses at least ten words)
20–36 months	uses toilet

All children will progress through these milestones at their own individual rates. However, significant failure to meet several of these milestones at the appropriate age may be an indication that a child has a developmental delay or mental retardation.

Infants born with mental retardation may appear to be less aware or less interested in their surroundings than are other babies. Just because a child may seem to be less responsive, however, does not mean the child is not learning

Crawling is another developmental milestone.

and shouldn't receive as much attention. All children learn at different rates—some faster and some slower than others. A child with mental retardation may not have her first smile at the same age as other children; she may not learn to crawl, walk, or talk as early as other children; but almost all children, even children with the most severe forms of mental retardation, will reach these important developmental stages. When a child smiles later than other children, her smile is no less special and important.

Every child has a right to . . . find its own way.
—George Bernard Shaw

3

I Want Ice Cream, Too

Krista slipped Penelope's stocking feet into the denim overalls. "Okay, stand up," she coaxed. Penelope tugged with short, chubby fingers on Krista's arm until she stood. Krista pulled up the overalls and fastened the silver snaps.

"Good job," she praised. "Let's get breakfast." She took Penelope's hand and walked slowly toward the kitchen, Penelope tripping over her feet along the way.

"What do you want to drink, Pen?" Krista hoisted the little girl into her high chair.

"Juice," Penelope signed with her hands.

"Okay. Say it first," Krista responded.

"Duce!" Penelope spat enthusiastically, throwing both arms into the air, happy with her accomplishment.

"That's right. Good job, Pen. Now say the whole thing," Krista began the ritual with patience, "I . . . waaannnt . . ."

"I waan duce!" Penelope raised her arms again and puffed out her chest with pride.

"Hey, good job." Krista laughed and gave her sister a hug. "You're fast this morning." Krista turned to the refrigerator, poured her sister a cup of orange juice, and took two medicine bottles from the cupboard. She broke apart the little caplets and mixed the powder into the juice before attaching the spill-free lid and handing the cup to her sister. "Now be careful," she warned as Penelope clumsily

49

seized the cup with both hands. "Drink it all." Penelope always had to drink all her juice so that she'd get all her medicine.

While Penelope drank, Krista made oatmeal. It was nine o'clock. Her parents were at work and her brothers had already left for school. After the oatmeal cooled, she spooned it carefully into Penelope's mouth until Penelope grimaced.

"No," Penelope signed. Krista looked down at the bowl. It was half empty; that wasn't so bad.

"Say it," she told Penelope.

"No mo." Penelope shook her head for emphasis.

"All right, no more, all done." Krista dumped the rest of the oatmeal down the sink. "Let's wash up and go." She wet a washcloth and rubbed the smears of oatmeal from Penelope's mouth. Penelope squirmed and contorted her face with displeasure. Krista reached down and tickled the little girl to distract her. Penelope laughed aloud.

"Tu-tu-tuckle!" she squealed as Krista lifted her from the high chair.

"That's right, I tickled you." Krista laughed as she readied her sister for the car.

Krista drove her sister to kindergarten every weekday morning. They picked up three other children along the way. Released from the car, the other children bounded toward the school entrance. Penelope, however, waited for Krista to unhook her and lift her from the car. Once free, Penelope gripped Krista's hand for balance as she teetered toward the door. At the classroom entrance, Krista knelt down and gave Penelope the daily directions.

"Pen, after school, Mrs. Peterson is going to pick you up and take you home, okay?" Penelope's eyes strayed to the other children, and Krista had to regain her attention. "Do you know who Mrs. Peterson is?" Krista asked.

"Back haiw." Penelope raised a finger to her mouth.

"That's right. Mrs. Peterson has black hair. So you'll go with Mrs. Peterson, okay?" Penelope made a face and stuck out her tongue. "Hey, be nice," Krista warned. Penelope retracted her tongue. "Good girl, I'll see you this afternoon." Krista kissed Penelope on the forehead and returned to her car.

On the way to her class, Krista contemplated how much her life had changed in the past five years. Five years ago, it pained her to remember, she had just been a selfish kid. Now she had graduated from college and spent her mornings dressing and feeding her little sister, participating in kindergarten car pool, and studying for her master's degree in special education.

Krista felt like Penelope had taught her to be a better person. It was from Penelope, in fact, that Krista had learned she wanted to be a special education teacher. Her first year in college, Krista had taken a class in sign language. When Penelope had trouble learning to talk, Krista started using the signs she'd learned to talk to Penelope. Soon Penelope was talking back! The Browns couldn't believe it. They had spent almost three years without hearing their little daughter speak, and now she was suddenly able to communicate. She couldn't say complicated things, of course, but just being able to communicate basic needs made a huge difference in Penelope's life and in her confidence. Seeing the way Penelope blossomed and changed once she could communicate made Krista want to become a special education teacher. Not everyone, she knew, had families as helpful, loving, and supportive as her own. She wanted to help those children so that they could achieve and grow like Penelope. Things were definitely difficult a lot of the time, but through watching Penelope grow Krista felt she was learning how truly wonderful and fulfilling life could be.

That afternoon, Krista drove home quickly. Her classes had run late. She hated to be late when Penelope got home, because then Penelope had to wait at the neighbor's house and this made Penelope nervous. When Krista did reach the house, she was surprised to see Mrs. Peterson's car still parked in the driveway. Mrs. Peterson and the kindergarten children stood in frantic postures around the driveway, but Penelope was nowhere to be seen. Fear rose in Krista's chest as she pulled up to Mrs. Peterson's car and stepped out.

"What happened? Where's Penelope?"

Exasperated, Mrs. Peterson waved an arm. "In there!" She pointed toward the car. "She's locked the doors and refuses to come out!"

Krista peered through the tinted windows to see Penelope curled up on the back seat crying. She tapped on the glass, but Penelope did not turn around.

"Well, what on earth happened?" Krista suspected that Mrs. Peterson or one of the children had done something to make Penelope upset. The other children milled round the car looking bored and tired.

"Nothing happened," Mrs. Peterson replied defensively. "I got out of the car to help Penelope out of her seat, but she refused to budge. She started kicking at me and crying when I tried to lift her out. So I told the other kids to get out of the car. I thought if everyone was out, she'd get out too, but when we walked away from the car and called her, she pulled the door closed and locked it." Mrs. Peterson's face turned red as she spoke. A curl of graying hair had come undone and hung limply in front of her right eye. "We've been here for nearly an hour!"

Krista tried to keep from rolling her eyes. She could just imagine Mrs. Peterson walking away from the car and calling Penelope: "Here Penelope, come here." And the children joining in the chorus, as if Penelope were a dog. People like Mrs. Peterson made Krista so angry sometimes.

"Did you try asking her what was wrong?" Krista tried to keep her voice calm.

Mrs. Peterson blinked, then narrowed her eyes. "There was nothing wrong, Krista." Mrs. Peterson spat out Krista's name as if it were a sour taste. "She's just being stubborn."

Krista turned her back on Mrs. Peterson and tapped on the car window again. This time Penelope looked up, her eyes puffy from crying and her face streaked with tears.

"Can I come in?" Krista signed. On the other side of the glass, Penelope looked doubtful. "Please?"

Penelope wiped her nose with the back of her hand, then sat up and reached for the door. When the door was unlocked, Krista slid in beside her sister. Inside, the car was stifling; Krista was amazed her sister had stood out against the heat this long. Outside the car, Mrs. Peterson watched them with a chilly glare and tapped her foot in rhythm to her displeasure.

"Hey, sweetie," Krista began, "can you tell me what happened? Why won't you get out of the car?" Penelope's face twisted at Krista's questions as though she might start crying again.

"I . . . I . . ." Penelope began, her breath broken by hiccupping gasps. Krista waited patiently for Penelope to continue. Mrs. Peterson tapped her foot louder while the children outside the car began to whine. Frustrated, Penelope gave up the attempt to speak and returned to signing. "I want ice cream, too," she told her sister.

"You want ice cream, too?" Krista repeated. Penelope nodded her head vigorously, her bottom lip trembling. "What ice cream?" Mrs. Peterson's foot stopped tapping, and a child's voice piped up behind Krista.

"Mrs. Peterson is taking us for ice cream," the little boy chimed. Beginning to understand what was going on, Krista turned a questioning look on Mrs. Peterson. Mrs. Peterson seemed to take a step back.

"I told the other kids we'd go out for ice cream after I dropped off Penelope." Krista's eyes widened and Mrs. Peterson looked uncomfortable. "Well, I didn't think she could understand me."

"Well, she's not stupid." Krista controlled her urge to jump out of the car and hit Mrs. Peterson. "How can you do that to a little kid? Talking in front of her as if she isn't even there?" Mrs. Peterson's mouth opened and closed, but no sound came out. The other children stood tense and silent, enthralled by the scene the two adults were making. Penelope began to cry again.

Krista turned back to her sister. "Hey, hey, hey," she coaxed, smoothing Penelope's hair. "Penny, look what I have." Krista pulled her cell phone, a contraption that Penelope loved, from her pocket. Penelope's eyes lit on the phone, but she did not stop crying. "I have a good idea, Pen." Krista flipped open the phone. "Why don't we call Phillip? We'll go see him at his apartment, and then we'll make him take us for ice cream."

Though the tears slowed, Penelope looked unsure. Krista continued speaking as she dialed the phone. "We can even stop at the high school and get Jonathan out of class. We'll take him with us, okay?" Penelope was looking more interested. "We'll go for ice cream, just you, me, Phillip, and Jonathan."

As the phone began to ring, Penelope nodded her head in agreement with the proposal and wrapped her arms around her sister's neck. With the phone cradled between her shoulder and ear, Krista slid across the seat and lifted her sister out of the hot car. Mrs. Peterson did not look at Krista or Penelope as she piled the rest of the children back into the car. Without a word of apology, she turned the key in the ignition.

"Hello," Phillip's voice answered on the other end of the phone.

"Hi, Phil," Krista responded as Penelope's face brightened. "Pen and I need you to take us for ice cream."

"Anything for my favorite sisters," Phillip responded as Mrs. Peterson pulled away.

SPEAKING IN SIGNS

People with mental retardation may take longer to learn language than other people. Sometimes, they may also have physical conditions that make it harder to speak so that others can understand. The early years can be frustrating for children with these conditions, especially if they can understand everything that is being said, but not be able to respond.

Sometimes sign language is a useful tool for children who are having trouble learning how to talk. Most sign language is not as complicated as spoken languages are, so it may be easier for young children or children with mental retardation to use while they are learning to perfect their speaking abilities. You can see, however, that Krista encourages Penelope to speak aloud. This is because Penelope will

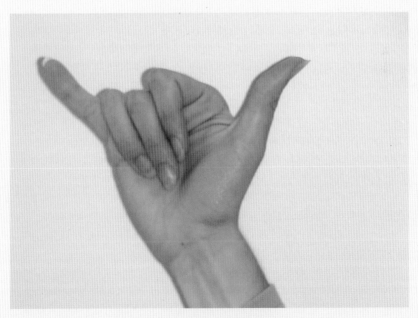

Sign language provides another communication option for individuals who have difficulty learning to speak.

be able to speak; it's just taking her a little while to learn. Krista doesn't want Penelope's use of sign language to discourage Penelope from talking. Krista also gives Penelope lots of encouragement, letting her know that she's done a good job when she says something correctly. Like most children with mental retardation who use sign language, once Penelope masters her **oral communication** skills, she will give up using sign language.

CAN PEOPLE WITH MENTAL RETARDATION GO TO SCHOOL?

Parents will decide to educate their children in different ways, but almost all people with mental handicaps can go to school and will benefit from doing so.

In school, most students with mental retardation will have some special classes that are designed to meet their specific needs. For example, many children with mental retardation will spend part of their school day with a speech therapist who will help them improve their speaking abilities. Most people with mental retardation will also have a special education teacher who helps them with different areas of learning and with **social skills**. A child with mental retardation or other special needs may even have physical or occupational therapists to give him special education in movement. Physical therapists help people with things like walking and standing while occupational therapists help people work on smaller muscle movements like using one's hands and fingers to dress and perform other tasks of daily living.

The United States government has laws that require schools to provide children with mental retardation and other special needs with the help and programs they need to learn. One of these laws is called the Individuals with Disabilities Education Act (or IDEA). Laws like IDEA are meant to

Children who are mentally retarded will receive special help at
school.

assure that all people with special needs are able to get the best education available. However, laws are constantly changing, and different people have different ideas about the best way to provide education to children. Sometimes, especially when there is a slow economy and the government wishes to reduce its spending, politicians try to change the laws that protect people with disabilities and attempt to cut the funding that the government provides for special education programs. Without funding, however, these programs can't exist and people with special needs can't get the education they deserve. **Activists** and **civil rights** organizations are always watching the laws and how they are changing and fighting to make sure people with special needs have **access** to a proper education.

Federal laws guarantee each child a "free and appropriate" education. Each state and school system has their own procedure for carrying out these laws, but basically IDEA guarantees that the following steps will take place:

1. *Search*. Each school system will have a procedure for identifying students who might have a disability that impacts their learning.
2. *Find*. Once a student with a potential problem has been identified, a system is in place for collecting information and designing an evaluation.
3. *Evaluation*. A comprehensive and multidisciplinary evaluation should be done. This will involve the school psychologist as well as teachers and other school personnel.
4. *Conference*. Parents or guardians meet with school personnel to review the evaluation conclusions, any labels or diagnoses established, any proposed placement, and the individualized education plan (IEP). All this should be recorded in writing.

5. *Parents' decision process.* Parents or guardians decide to accept, request explanations or changes, or reject the proposed placement and IEP.
6. *Appeals process.* If parents reject the label or diagnosis, placement recommendation, or IEP, an appeals process starts with the local school and can go from there to the county or state level.
7. *Follow-up.* Progress reports are provided to the family at least annually, and a formal reevaluation is done every three years (or sooner if requested by parents or teachers). Steps 5 and 6 are then repeated before implementing the next year's plans.

Every child in the United States is guaranteed a "free and appropriate" education.

A child who is mentally retarded may benefit from teaching techniques that allow him to explore and learn by using his hands.

Individualized Education Plan (IEP)

An IEP is a written plan designed specifically for each child in need of special education. It defines reasonable expectations for achievement and how success will be determined. It should include these points:

1. A statement of the child's current level of education performance.
2. A statement of yearly goals or achievements expected for each area of identified weakness by the end of the school year.
3. Short-term objectives stated in instructional terms (concrete, observable steps leading to the mastery of the yearly goals).
4. A statement of the specific special education and support services to be provided to the child.
5. A statement of the extent to which a child will be able to participate in regular education programs and justification for any special placement recommended.
6. Projected dates for the beginning of services and how long they are anticipated to last.
7. A statement of the criteria and evaluation procedures to be used in determining (on at least an annual basis, if not more frequently) whether the short-term objectives have been achieved.

PAINFUL MISUNDERSTANDINGS

Sometimes, when people speak in front of a child with mental retardation, they may act as if the child isn't even present. Unfortunately, this mistake is common. Many people assume that just because a child with mental retardation might communicate differently or might not communicate as well as other

Children who are mentally retarded enjoy and learn from opportunities to socialize with other children.

people, the person must not understand what is being said. People may think that the child is misbehaving or being stubborn. What might have actually happened, however, was that a person did something very hurtful to the child, and the child was having trouble communicating her feelings. Like many people, the child is able to understand far more than she can communicate. She is not "stupid." She knows that everyone else is being invited to go have fun and that she is being left out because she is different.

This type of scenario is all too common in the lives of people with mental retardation. It is wrong to exclude people with mental retardation from regular activities, to assume that they can't understand what is going on around them, or to think that they don't have the same emotions as other people. People with mental retardation can participate in the same activities, understand many of the same situations, and feel the same emotions as other people.

Each day . . . learn something new.
—Solon

4

A Fish in the Water

Penelope dove beneath the surface of the water and swam toward her brother's legs. They looked funny and wavy through her goggles. A mist of bubbles tumbled through the water, obscuring her view. She popped her head above the surface to get a breath, then plunged forward again.

Swimming was Penelope's favorite activity. Phillip, who had won various trophies and awards for swimming, had shared his love of the water with his sister. When Penelope was smaller, he took her to the pool all the time and taught her how to swim. But now he was older and had an important job and lived in an apartment, so they only went swimming together on Saturdays.

Penelope rose for another breath and swam forward harder. Her brother's legs seemed to be getting further away. She reached for them, but they sidestepped her grab, startling her to the surface.

"Hey, you're cheating!" Water rushed into Penelope's mouth.

"No, I'm not," Phillip laughed. "You're just too slow to catch me." Penelope gasped at her brother's words, her smile turning immediately into a frown.

"Phillip," Penelope pleaded, "I'm not slow." It was almost a question more than it was a statement.

Phillip shook his head at his own words. He couldn't believe he'd said something so unkind. After all these years, he thought he knew better than to say things like that. At school, kids had a fondness for taunting Penelope by calling her Slowpoke Penny or by just calling her Slow, as if it were her name. Penelope had developed a special dislike for the word in any way it was used.

"Pen, I'm sorry." Phillip took Penelope's arm, trying to undo the damage he'd just done. "I didn't mean it that way. I was just fooling around. You know I think you're fast. You're a fast swimmer, just like me." Penelope seemed to like being compared with her brother, but she was still reluctant to believe him too easily. She looked up to where her parents sat in the gallery over the pool.

"Do you think I'm a fast swimmer, Dad?"

"You're a faster swimmer than I'll ever be, Pen," Mr. Brown called down.

Penelope smiled. "Well, that's for sure," she said and gave her hiccupping laugh. "Do you think I'm a fast swimmer, Mom?"

"You're just like a fish in the water," Mrs. Brown yelled down. The other children at the pool turned their heads and observed the exchange, but none of the Browns seemed to notice.

"A fish!" Penelope guffawed loudly. Turning to her brother, she laughed. "Mom called me a fish!" Seeing that no harm had been done, Phillip laughed as well.

"So, Pen, I've been thinking." Phillip was eager to change the subject. "You should join the Special Olympics."

"What's special limpis?"

"Well, it's a group of people who play sports. Some people run. Some people ski. Some people swim. But everyone is special. They're all people that were made differently, like you." Phillip paused, hoping he was explaining it in a way that Penelope would understand, but that wouldn't hurt her feelings. But Penelope didn't seem hurt at all.

"Everyone's like me?" she questioned wide-eyed. "Will I make friends?"

"Yes, you'll make lots of friends," Phillip encouraged.

"Why don't we go before?" Penelope's voice sounded amazed.

"You weren't old enough to go before, but now you're eight. Now you're old enough to go."

Penelope laughed and jumped with excitement. She clapped her hands, sending water squirting into Phillip's eye. He laughed and splashed Penelope back.

As Penelope and Phillip laughed and splashed each other, a boy exited the locker room and walked toward the pool. Penelope watched the boy as he came to the water's edge. As he stepped into the water, Penelope pointed toward the boy and said, "He's fat, isn't he Phillip?" She spoke loudly and many people turned their heads in the direction of the boy. The boy glanced up toward Penelope, then looked away, obviously embarrassed, trying to pretend he hadn't heard.

"Penelope, don't point," Phillip told her sternly. "Don't say things like that about people." Penelope dropped her hand, but looked surprised.

"Why not? He is fat." Her voice was just as loud as before. More heads turned to watch Penelope, and Mr. and Mrs. Brown sat uncomfortably in the balcony, observing Phillip's handling of the situation.

"Come here, Pen," Phillip said more gently, guiding Penelope by the hand to the side of the pool. Phillip felt like he'd had this conversation with his sister a thousand times, but he guessed they'd just have to have it again. "Pen, you know how I've told you before that we can't always say everything we think?" Penelope looked at her brother, but made no movement. "I say 'think before you speak,' right?" Penelope nodded. "Now you know how you feel when people call you slow?" Phillip wished he didn't have to remind her, but he knew it had to be done. Penelope looked away from her brother's eyes and gazed down at the bottom of the pool. Phillip waited for a sign that she was still listening, and when she didn't give one, he gently placed a finger beneath her chin and lifted her face back toward his own. "Well, that's the way you made that boy feel by calling him fat."

Tears welled in Penelope's eyes and jerked at Phillip's heart. "I didn't want to make him sad," Penelope sniffled, swallowing the hiccups in her throat.

"I know you didn't, Pen," Phillip said soothingly, "but you have to go over to the boy and say that you're sorry, okay?" Penelope looked back down at the water. Phillip raised her chin again. "Okay?" he questioned a little more firmly.

Penelope turned reluctantly away from Phillip and swam slowly toward the boy who was still sitting, head lowered at the side of the pool. When she got to his side, she raised her chubby hand to his knee. The boy kept his eyes averted as Penelope spoke.

"I'm sorry," she said in her slow, careful speech. "I didn't want to make you sad." The boy didn't look at Penelope, but he shrugged his shoulders.

"That's okay," was his only reply. He hopped down into the water and swam away.

THE SPECIAL OLYMPICS

Just because people may have disabilities or special needs doesn't mean that they can't participate in sports. Swimming is a very good type of exercise because people with Down syndrome may have trouble with their muscles, bones, and joints. Swimming is a great way to strengthen your muscles without harming your bones and joints.

The Special Olympics is an international organization that has allowed many people with mental retardation to become athletes, travel, have fun, and lead happier, healthier lives. The Special Olympics helps more than one million people in over 150 countries around the world. In the Special Olympics, there are no losers, only winners. Everyone who competes wins a ribbon. Some of the sports that Special Olympians can compete in are:

- badminton
- basketball
- bowling
- cross-country skiing
- downhill skiing
- figure skating
- golf
- gymnastics
- horseback riding
- roller-skating
- snowboarding
- snowshoeing
- soccer
- softball
- speed skating
- swimming
- volleyball

KNOWING WHAT TO SAY AND
WHEN TO SAY IT

Communicating with other people is not always easy. In some situations it can be very difficult to know what is the proper thing to say and when is the proper time to say it. Social skills are some of the things that we learn as we mature. Just as people with mental retardation may take longer to learn certain things in school, they may also take longer to learn certain social skills. They may not always say the right things at the right times. In other situations, a person may know the right thing to say but may say it in the wrong way. For example, if a child needed to use the rest room, telling his parents of his need might be the right thing to say, but shouting it loudly in the middle of a quiet library would be the wrong way to say it.

Communication is an important skill.

Students with mental retardation learn self-defense skills while they also practice getting along with others.

People with mental retardation often need extra help learning how to interact socially. Sometimes, the best teachers of proper social interaction are our **peers**. Many people think that it is best for people with mental retardation to study in regular classrooms along with students who don't have mental retardation. In this setting, children will learn much about proper behavior from their peers. However, it's also important that family members and teachers give children proper guidance and correct discipline. Family members and teachers should gently point out when a child makes a mistake, explain why the action was wrong, coach the child on how to correct the action, and then make sure the child follows through.

Sometimes people think it is better to just let a child with mental retardation make mistakes and not point out those

Students with mental retardation enjoy taking part in their school's prom.

mistakes. However, this is not a good way to raise any child. Think how difficult it would be for you to learn, grow, and improve yourself if no one ever told you when you were wrong and how to fix your mistakes. Children with mental retardation and other special needs deserve the same chances as everyone else to improve themselves. On the other hand, sometimes parents try to shelter their children from mistakes and failure. They may prevent their child from doing anything because they are afraid that if their child does something wrong, she will feel hurt or embarrassed. Parents shouldn't allow mistakes to slip by uncorrected, but they also shouldn't prevent the child from trying new things and making mistakes. It is often through makings mistakes that we learn; change our behavior; and then, when our changed behavior leads to success, find new confidence. Just like everyone else, children with mental retardation need encouragement, correction, support, and the freedom to make mistakes in order to learn and grow.

My friend is one . . . who takes me for what I am.
—Henry David Thoreau

5

SOME PEOPLE
DO BAD THINGS

Penelope loved Special Olympics. She still liked to go swimming
with Phillip—no one could make her laugh the way Phillip
could—but in some ways, Special Olympics was even more fun.
People always cheered for her at the Special Olympics races, and not
just her mom and dad either, but lots of people. She now had a
whole wall of ribbons in her bedroom, just like Phillip's wall of trophies! It made her feel proud to look at the layers upon layers of
silken ribbons. It made her feel like she could do anything.

But at Special Olympics, Penelope had something even better
than cheers and ribbons: She had friends. Of course she had some
friends at school, but at school there were also people who sometimes made fun of her. At Special Olympics everyone was like her.
They were real friends who knew her name and that she was ten
years old, knew that she liked bananas, that her favorite color was
sparkly gold, and that she loved her swimming cap so much she
sometimes wore it to bed. Penelope knew all kinds of things about
her friends as well. She knew that Jason loved baseball cards and lol-
lipops and that he hurt his head when he was a little baby—that's
why he walked and talked funny. She knew that Sara could ride a
bike real well, but took a long time to say her s's, and t's, but it was
okay, because if you were just patient, Sara would say what she
wanted to say. Penelope also knew that Sara came to Special Olympics because her mother had been very sick before Sara was born.
Sara had been on a roller coaster once, which made her throw up,

75

and she had an older stepbrother Sam, whom she didn't like at all. It was fun to know so many things about her friends and to have friends who knew things about her. Penelope definitely thought that Special Olympics was the best place in the world.

Today was an especially exciting day, because Sara's mom was letting Sara go home with Penelope after swimming. Penelope could barely contain her excitement. She'd never had a friend spend the night at her house before. Her mom and dad had planned all kinds of great things. Her dad was going to make his special banana cream pie, Penelope's favorite, and her mom was going to help them build a fort in the living room. Her parents were even going to let them stay up late, just like big kids. And Jonathan promised that the next day, he would take Penelope and Sara to his college and show them how to make pots by spinning clay around on a wheel. Penelope and Sara were so excited they could barely concentrate on swimming!

The first part of the evening was great. Phillip and Krista came over for dinner, and Penelope and Sara laughed and laughed as Phillip pretended to put food in Krista's hair. After Phillip and Krista left, Penelope's mom helped the girls build the best fort ever and showed them how to use their flashlights to make their faces turn red. This made them giggle when Penelope's mom was around, but after Mr. and Mrs. Brown went to bed, Penelope and Sara thought the red faces were kind of scary, so they propped the flashlights together in the middle of the fort instead, the rays of light shining up like a campfire illuminating their living-room wilderness.

Once Mr. and Mrs. Brown went to bed and the other lights went out, however, Sara began to tell a story that confused and troubled Penelope.

"Penelope," Sara began in her small, quiet voice, "I think I am vewy bad."

"Why do you think that, Sara?" Penelope's curiosity was roused.

"Because of Sssssss-s-s . . ." Sara got hung up on a stutter. Penelope waited patiently for her friend to find the word she was looking for. Penelope didn't mind the way Sara talked. In fact she liked it. It was like listening to popcorn popping. Sara found the word. "Ss-s-s-Sam. We do things that would make Mom angry."

"What kind of things?" Penelope asked. Sara stared into the glowing flashlights and hesitated. Her mouth worked on words, but nothing came out. Finally she asked a very difficult question.

"Ss-s-s-s-Sam t-tells me t-t-to t-t-touch him," Sara stuttered, her words jerking and popping. Penelope felt confused.

"Is that bad?"

Nodding her head solemnly, Sara bit her lip as tears welled in her eyes. "Ss-some t-t-times . . ." Sara seemed to be having even more trouble than usual getting her words out. Her whole body seemed rigid in an attempt to force out the syllables. "Ss-s-some t-t-times he t-tells me t-to—" Sara took a deep shaky breath, and then her final words came out in a sudden stream. Tears slid down Sara's cheeks, and she lowered her eyes to avoid Penelope's confused look. Penelope thought the story sounded strange, and Sara's emotions frightened her. She didn't know why it would make Sara bad, but Sara seemed to think it did.

"Well," Penelope began thoughtfully, looking for something to help her friend, "can't you tell him to stop doing that?"

"No." Her voice was barely more than a whisper, and Penelope had to struggle to hear what her friend was saying. "Ss-s-Sam ss-s-says he'll t-t-tell my mom and that she won't love me anymore."

Penelope was horrified by her friend's statement. It sounded like the worst thing that could ever happen. Sara gulped big breaths of air. Anguish twisted her face as she pulled at her hair with nervous fingers. Penelope searched for something that would make her friend feel better. She suddenly didn't want to talk about this uncomfortable subject anymore.

"Let's go eat more banana cream pie," Penelope suggested. She took Sara's hand and led her out of the fort and into the kitchen.

THE IMPORTANCE OF FRIENDS

Special Olympics is a wonderful place, not only because it provides exercise and confidence, but also because it is a place where people can get together and have fun. Sometimes it is difficult for people with mental retardation and other forms of disabilities to make friends. People who don't have disabilities may feel uncomfortable, not know what to say, or just plain be mean to people with disabilities. For many people, before joining Special Olympics, their only friends are family members. Supportive family members are very important, but most people with mental retardation want to have friends outside their family like other people have. Friends bring joy to our lives, give us people to share our experiences with, and teach us about others and our-

Special Olympics provide an opportunity for children with mental retardation to enjoy competition, achievement, and social interaction.

People with mental retardation can become skilled swimmers.

selves. Friends are just as important to people with mental retardation as to anybody else.

Some people especially like Special Olympics because they are able to meet friends who are like themselves. Some may have suffered a **traumatic** brain injury when they were young or others had a mother who was sick when she was pregnant. Both traumatic brain injury and illness of a pregnant mother or a young child can cause mental retardation. In fact, there are many different things like illnesses, injuries, and genetic conditions that can lead to mental retardation.

Although one may find comfort by spending time with people like oneself, it is not always good for people to only have friends who are like themselves. It is good to have all different kinds of friends—not just friends with disabilities like one's own or just friends without disabilities. Perhaps you have never thought of being friends with a person who has mental retardation. You might think that you would have nothing in common. But people with mental retardation have likes, dislikes, talents, dreams, and things to talk about just like any other person. By focusing on the things you have in common rather than on your differences, you can have friendships with all kinds of people. Many people without mental retardation have very important and fulfilling friendships with people who have disabilities.

SPEECH IMPAIRMENTS

Many people stutter or have other forms of speech impairment; just because someone has difficulty speaking correctly does not mean he has mental retardation. However, such speech impairments are also very common among people with mental disabilities. A person may stutter when she tries to say certain sounds, and her stuttering grows worse when she is tense or tired.

Many people get tense when they hear a person stutter, tell the person to "spit out the word," or do things like look at their watch or roll their eyes to show that they are frustrated. It is important to remember that the person stuttering is much more frustrated than the listener, and showing impatience will only make the speaker feel worse. The person who stutters cannot help it when she stutters. The best thing to do is to wait patiently for the person to finish the words she's trying to say.

SOME PEOPLE DO BAD THINGS

Stories of sexual abuse are frightening. Often people do not know what to think or how to react. And unfortunately, this is far too common among children, especially children with mental retardation or other disabilities.

People who are mentally retarded can be good friends.

The abused child may think that this makes her bad or that the abuse is her fault. Of course, when sexual abuse happens, it is never the abused person's fault. Even if the abused person knows that the abuse is wrong or thinks that she is somehow responsible for making the abuse happen, it is still important for that person to know that it is not her fault.

Sometimes an abused child is threatened that if she tells her parents, they won't love her anymore. This is certainly not true, but children may not know what to think or how to stop the abuse. Sometimes people who sexually abuse other people will abuse people with mental retardation. They think that the person with mental retardation will not know what is happening or will not be able to tell others or get help to make it stop. Maybe they even think that other people won't believe someone with mental retardation who says she was abused. Parents, school officials, medical workers, counselors, and police officers are some of the people who can help an individual find out how to make the abuse stop.

THE HISTORY OF MENTAL RETARDATION

In Europe in the fourteenth and fifteenth centuries, the mentally retarded were sometimes looked upon as "holy infants" blessed by God. However, during the Reformation, Martin Luther referred to mentally retarded people as "feeble-minded" and "Godless"; he wrote that society should rid themselves of the burden of these people. In France in the early twentieth century, Alfred Binet was the first to develop psychometric tests that attempted to measure human intellectual capacity. Although these tests may have been designed with noble intentions, they were often used to identify "imbeciles" and exclude these children from school. In 1934, Foling discovered **phenylketonuria**, one cause of mental retardation. Phenylketonuria happens to be treatable; as a result, for the first time the scientific study of mental retardation became "respectable."

We hold these truths to be self-evident;
that all [people] are created equal. . . .
—Declaration of Independence

6

MY NAME IS NOT SLOW

Penelope knew she looked beautiful in the purple satin dress. It was the nicest thing she'd ever worn. She looked in the mirror as her mother tied white flowers in her hair and thought how pretty she looked and how surprised all the boys at the high school would be if they saw her right now.

"I look pretty, don't I," she said to her mother, though it wasn't a question. Mrs. Brown smiled down at her youngest daughter. "You sure do, Pen. You look beautiful."

The church looked beautiful too. The same white flowers adorning Penelope's hair were mirrored everywhere. It was Krista's wedding day, and Penelope was the maid of honor.

"But not as pretty as Krista," Penelope informed her mother seriously.

"No," Mrs. Brown smiled. "The bride has to be the prettiest on her wedding day."

Penelope couldn't wait to see Krista in her long, white dress. She had helped Krista pick it out. In fact, she had helped with the wedding a lot. She and Jonathan had made all the invitations together. And she and Phillip had gone to different restaurants to find the best one for the party afterward. It had been a lot of work, and now that the day was finally here, she could barely contain her excitement.

Mrs. Brown left the room to get more hairpins. As she swung through the door, another purple-clad bridesmaid came bouncing in. It was Jennifer, Krista's best friend from college. Penelope had known Jennifer for years, and she thought Jennifer was pretty good to talk to.

"Are you excited, Penelope?"

"Oh, yes!" Penelope leaned close to the mirror and fumbled a tube of mascara with her short fingers. Jennifer watched for a moment, then decided she should help.

"Would you like help with your makeup, Penelope?" she offered.

Penelope looked at Jennifer with suspicion. "Will you make me pretty?" she asked.

"Well of course I will, silly," Jennifer smiled. Penelope smiled as well and relinquished the mascara to Jennifer's more experienced hand. Not needing to concentrate on the makeup so hard, Penelope was free to talk.

"Will Krista have babies now that she is married?" she asked Jennifer, hoping the answer was yes.

"Probably. I don't know." Jennifer shrugged her shoulders.

"Well, doesn't everyone have babies when they get married?" Her voice showed her disappointment.

"Lots of people do." Jennifer powdered Penelope's nose with a big, soft puff of cotton. "But not everyone who gets married has babies," Jennifer paused, "and not everyone who has babies gets married." She shrugged her shoulders again feeling that she'd given a pretty good explanation. Penelope seemed satisfied with this explanation as well. The powder tickled in her nose, and she thought that she might sneeze.

"Okay, make your lips go like this." Jennifer opened her mouth and stretched her lips. Penelope mimicked the movement and Jennifer began drawing waxy lipstick across her mouth.

"When I'm married, I'm going to have babies," Penelope told Jennifer confidently, the lipstick getting wavy on her mouth as she spoke. Jennifer stopped and looked up. She closed the lipstick with a snap, and Penelope wondered if she'd done something wrong. Jennifer, seeming uncomfortable, pulled a tissue from the nearby box and began to gently blot Penelope's lips.

"Penelope," she spoke slowly, her voice dripping with a tone Penelope did not like, "you know you can't get married." Penelope pulled back from Jennifer's dabbing hand.

"Why not?"

"Well because, honey—" Jennifer paused and appeared to search for words. "Because you're slow."

Penelope shrank away from Jennifer's words. "My name is not Slow," she mumbled in a hurt tone. "My name is Pen-el-o-pe." She annunciated each syllable as if the word was difficult to understand. Jennifer rolled her eyes.

"I know your name, silly." Jennifer's voice now hinted annoyance. "You know what I mean. You can't get married because you're retarded."

Penelope's gut wrenched. She stared into Jennifer's eyes, but Jennifer was unyielding. "I'm sorry, honey, but that's just the way it is." Jennifer gave one last shrug before standing and swishing back out the room.

As Jennifer passed through the doors, Mrs. Brown returned, hairpins in hand. She could tell by the static-like tension in the room that something had happened. Penelope's shoulders slumped and her eyes looked watery, but Mrs. Brown couldn't get her to reveal what had transpired.

For the entire ceremony, Penelope stood, shifting her weight from foot to foot, tears running down her face, trying to avoid looking at Jennifer who stood right beside her. Penelope usually loved to dance, but at the reception, Jonathan couldn't get her to leave her seat. Mr. and Mrs. Brown watched their daughter anxiously from the dance floor, and even Phillip failed to make her smile. Finally, Krista broke away from her groom to spend some time at Penelope's side. As she walked toward Penelope, the white dress they had chosen together swaying with her smooth, happy movements, Penelope began to cry even harder. Krista sat and put her arm around her sister.

"Hey, Pen, do you want to tell me what's wrong?" She smoothed Penelope's ruffled hair. Penelope squeezed her eyes shut and stubbornly shook her head. Krista gave her a little time to think before speaking again. "Well, you don't have to if you don't want to . . . but I think you'll feel better if you tell me what's wrong."

A sob broke from Penelope's lips as she began to speak. "Jennifer said I can't get married because I'm retarded." She coughed, the pain almost too much to bear.

Krista gasped. "Jennifer said that?"

Penelope nodded, then looked at Krista with trusting eyes. "Is it true?" Her question seemed to be a plea.

"No, Pen," Krista's words were firm. "No, that's not true. If you find someone you love and who loves you, you can get married, just like everyone else."

Penelope wasn't yet relieved. Her hands still twisted with anxiety. "And—" She seemed afraid to ask the question. "Can I have babies?"

Krista's heart skipped a beat. She hadn't realized that no one had explained these things to Penelope before. "Well, Pen, maybe . . . I don't know. Some people can have babies, and some people can't." Krista didn't know what else to say, and Penelope's stricken look returned.

"But how do I know what type of person I am?" she cried.

Krista thought a moment. She didn't feel qualified to say much more to her sister, but she had an idea. "How about this," she suggested. "Next time you go to see Dr. Rosa, I'll go with you and we'll ask her about seeing a special doctor who can tell you all about having babies. Would that help?"

Penelope thought about the suggestion. It seemed like a good one. After a moment, she wrapped her arms around her sister's neck. "Krista, you're so smart," Penelope whispered into her sister's ear. "You always know the right thing to say."

CAN PEOPLE WITH MENTAL RETARDATION GET MARRIED?

Many people think that individuals with mental retardation remain like children for their whole lives, but this is not true. People with mental retardation may learn many things slower than other people. They may also have delayed social and emotional development. But it is extremely important to remember that people with mental retardation grow up to be adults just like everybody else. As adults they will have adult interests in love, sex, marriage, and even childbearing.

In the past, both individuals and governments have tried to discourage people with mental retardation from having sex, getting married, or having children. In fact, many terrible things have been done to people with mental retardation to ensure that they do not have children. During the **Holocaust**, Adolf Hitler, the leader of the Nazi party in Germany, ordered that all people with mental retardation be **sterilized**. He then had doctors perform medical experiments on these people and even had people with mental retardation killed.

Hitler, however, was certainly not the first person to perform such crimes against people with mental retardation. In fact, similar crimes were being performed in the United States long before Hitler came to power in Germany. More than thirty U.S. states had **eugenics** programs, and more than sixty thousand people with mental disabilities were sterilized during this time. Today, more than thirty states still have laws that restrict marriage between two people who have mental retardation or even make such marriages illegal. Some people say these laws are meant to help people with intellectual disabilities. Other people say that the laws **infringe** on people's most basic human rights. These laws are still quite widespread. However, they are rarely enforced.

People with mental retardation can be good parents.

Individuals with mental retardation have normal urges to date and marry.

You may be surprised to know that many people with mental retardation do, in fact, get married. According to different studies, between 40 and 60 percent of all people with mental retardation do marry. About half of these people are married to other people who also have mental retardation.

Although the rates are smaller than those for marriage, many people with mental retardation also have children. Perhaps as many as 25 percent of people with mental retardation become parents. Some people's disabilities make it physically impossible for them to conceive or carry children to term. Other people have genetic disorders that can be passed to their children. However, the majority of children born to parents with mental retardation do not have mental retardation themselves.

Just because a person has mental retardation does not mean that she cannot be a good and loving parent. How-

A child with mental retardation benefits from opportunities to manipulate objects with her hands.

ever, there is a possibility that mothers and fathers with mental retardation will not always be aware of all of their child's needs. Therefore, parents with mental retardation may need extra help from their families, friends, and community and state organizations to help them meet all of their child's physical, emotional, and intellectual needs.

DIFFERENT LEVELS OF MENTAL RETARDATION

How well a person with mental retardation can cope with various life responsibilities will depend on the level of mental retardation. The DSM-IV recognizes four levels of mental retardation:

- mild mental retardation: IQ level 50–55 to approximately 70
- moderate retardation: IQ level 35–40 to 50–55
- severe mental retardation: IQ level 20–25 to 25–40
- profound mental retardation: IQ below 20 or 25

Students with moderate retardation may attend a special school or they may attend a special classroooom in a public school.

Mild Mental Retardation

Children who have this level of mental retardation will learn more slowly in school, but their disorder may not even be noticeable when they are in non-academic settings. As they grow older, they are capable of taking responsibility for their basic, day-to-day needs, and they usually develop adequate social and communication skills. By their late teens, they will generally reach approximately a sixth-grade level of academic achievement. Their choice of careers will be somewhat limited, but with adequate supervision and support from family or the community, they are capable of supporting themselves successfully. This is the level that would be

Children with mild mental retardation can usually attend regular elementary schools, although they will probably also receive special education services.

Students with moderate mental retardation learn very basic skills.

most apt to apply to Penelope. According to the DSM-IV, about 85 percent of all people diagnosed with mental retardation fall into this categoy.

Moderate Mental Retardation

Children with this level of mental retardation will usually learn the communication skills they need to interact with others. At the elementary school level, their programs will concentrate on the basic academic skills needed for daily life, such as reading, adding and subtracting, telling time, or handling money. These children are unlikely to go much past a second-grade level, and as they grow older, their school programs will be more apt to concentrate on basic self-help skills. As adults, vocationally they will generally do well in sheltered workshops or supervised work settings. Their home

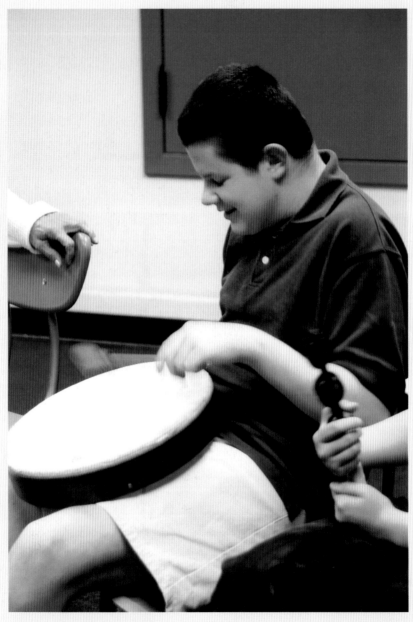

A student with moderate mental retardation enjoys playing the drum during music class.

life will generally need to be supervised, either by their family or an institutionalized community. The DSM-IV states that this level of mental retardation makes up about 9 to 11 percent of all people diagnosed with mental retardation.

Severe Mental Retardation

Somewhere between 35 and 60 percent of the people who function at this level of mental retardation have genetic reasons for their conditions. Children with severe mental retardation often have other disabilities as well (for example, physical disabilities or blindness). Their school programs will concentrate on basic self-care skills, communication, and

A student with severe mental retardation will benefit from recreational activities and other opportunities to learn social skills.

getting along appropriately with others. Their education may also include familiarity with the alphabet, simple counting, and some sight reading of important words like "exit," "men," "women," and "don't walk." As adults, these individuals will usually do well in supervised settings, either with their families or in **group homes**. In some cases, however, they may have an associated medical problem that will require them to live in a nursing facility. According to the DSM-IV, this group of individuals makes up about three to four percent of all people with mental retardation.

Classes for individuals with severe mental retardation may focus on activities that teach sorting skills while helping them develop better coordination of their hands.

Profound Mental Retardation

This level of the disorder is rare; only about one in every 2,000 children is profoundly retarded. According to the DSM-IV, most children who are diagnosed with this level of mental retardation have a **neurological** condition that accounts for their disorder. As young children, they will have obvious problems sensing the world around them, and they will have difficulty moving around. As they grow older, they will learn the most in a very structured environment where they have constant help and supervision from a caregiver. With this sort of training, their motor development, self-care, and ability to talk may improve. Eventually, as adults, they may be able to perform simple tasks in well-supervised work settings. About one to two percent of all people with mental retardation have this degree of difficulties.

Children learn at their own pace.
—Bertrand Russell

7

WHERE ARE YOU GOING, PHILLIP?

Penelope gently turned the knob and eased the door open inch by inch. Quietly, she snuck her head into the room and looked for Phillip. He was sitting on the balcony with a fuzzy blue blanket wrapped about his shoulders, serenely watching the city below. Penelope smiled and let herself into the room.

"Phillip!" Penelope bounded toward the balcony.

"What's that?" Phillip's back straightened and his head turned slowly above thin shoulders. "Is that my most favorite sister?" Penelope could hear the smile in his voice even though he spoke in barely a whisper.

"It is your most favoritest sister!" Penelope threw her hands into the air, then wrapped her arms around her brother's thin body. "You're getting hair again!" She observed as her cheek brushed against her brother's head.

"That's because they stopped giving me that strong medicine." Phillip smiled, taking his younger sister's hand. Dark moons appeared beneath his eyes, and his skin wrinkled as if he were very old. Penelope smiled back.

"That was bad medicine." She nodded gravely. It sounded like good news that Phillip wasn't taking the medicine that made his hair fall out anymore.

"That means you can grow your hair back, too, Baldy." Phillip lifted a limp hand and placed it on his sister's shaved head. "You look funny without hair, anyway." He forced the words out with a long, wheezing breath.

Penelope stuck out her bottom lip at her brother. When Phillip told her he was going to lose his hair, Penelope had said that she would cut her hair off, too. Phillip warned her that people might look at her funny if she did, but Penelope said that people had been looking at her funny for her whole life—she didn't care. Then everyone in the whole family decided to cut off their hair, even Penelope's mom and dad. They said they were doing it out of *solidarity* with Phillip. Penelope didn't know what that meant, but she knew that it had made Phillip laugh when she, Krista, Jonathan, Mom, and Dad had gathered in his hospital room and shaved their heads one by one. As the ringlets of hair floated through the air and the pile of locks grew upon the floor, Phillip laughed the way he used to laugh before he got sick, and that was a good sound.

Philip had been sick for a long time. Something was growing in his brain. Penelope couldn't remember what it was called, but she knew it made Phillip feel very bad. Sometimes he felt so bad that he didn't even know who his sister was. Those were bad days. But on good days, Phillip seemed just like his old self. Penelope was happy it was a good day, because she wanted to tell Phillip her exciting news.

"Phillip," she said in a voice bubbling with happiness, ignoring the fact that he'd called her Baldy, "guess what?"

"Um, Mom and Dad bought an elephant!" Phillip coughed. Penelope's eyes went wide at Phillip's suggestion. Phillip got a serious look on his face. "No? Not an elephant?" He sounded genuinely surprised. He thought for a moment, then his face lit up. "I've got it! Jonathan's going to fly around the world in a hot-air balloon!" A slow smile spread on his lips. Penelope looked at him with shock for a moment before Phillip's smile infected her own face.

"No silly!" she squealed. Her brother could be so ridiculous sometimes. "In three days, it's my birthday!"

"It is?" Phillip feigned surprise.

Penelope nodded her head enthusiastically. "And you know

what else? I'm going to be twenty-one years old! That's more than all my fingers and toes put together." She waved her hands for her brother to see. "And you know what else?" She barely paused for breath. Phillip shook his head. "Mom and Dad are going to throw me a big party, and Sara is going to come, and Jason is going to come, and Krista and her husband and Jonathan and even more people." Penelope threw up her palms to emphasize how big the gathering would be. Then she paused, becoming serious, "And you're going to come, too. Right, Phillip?"

The atmosphere on the balcony suddenly changed, the air getting heavy the way it does before rain. Phillip was quiet, no longer smiling, and Penelope began to nervously clasp and unclasp her hands. With effort, Phillip raised his own hands and placed them on Penelope's. "Pen," he spoke in soft, soothing tones, "Pen, I won't be able to come to your party." Tears began to form in Penelope's eyes, but somehow she was not surprised by what Phillip said.

"But why not?" she whispered. "Where are you going?" Phillip paused, a flash of pain moving like a shadow across his face before his usual look of serenity returned.

"You know what, Pen, before I tell you, can you do me a favor?" Penelope's head bounced up and down. She would do anything for Phillip. "Will you go down to the gift shop and buy me one of those floating balloons?" Penelope smiled. She often bought balloons for Phillip from the hospital gift shop.

When Penelope returned, a yellow balloon floating on the end of a long string, Phillip asked her to bring a chair out to the balcony and sit down next to him. Feeling that something big was about to happen, Penelope quietly obeyed. She handed the balloon to her brother, who watched it bouncing on the end of its string for a moment before he began to speak. Penelope sensed he was gathering his strength and waited patiently. She was suddenly very frightened. When Phillip finally spoke, it was without the rasping whisper that so often accompanied his voice. Instead his voice was pure and confident.

"Pen, did Mom and Dad tell you why the doctor stopped giving me that medicine?" Penelope shook her head no. Inwardly, Phillip's heart sank. Why did they insist on keeping these things from her? He regretted his parents' attempts to shield Penelope from the truth. What did they think was going to happen if they didn't tell her what was happening? He took a deep breath, trying to conceal his inward turmoil. It would only be harder for Penelope if she thought he was upset. "They stopped giving me the medicine because it wasn't working," Phillip stated as simply and matter-of-factly as he could. "Pen, I'm not going to get better."

Penelope blinked at her brother. What did he mean, not get better? How could he not get better? "You mean you're always going to be sick?" Her voice trembled.

Suddenly, Phillip felt very tired, but he knew he had to make Penelope understand. When he spoke again, the rasping whisper had returned to his voice. "No, Pen." He hesitated for a long time. "I mean I'm dying."

Penelope stared at her brother. He was so thin and small that the blanket appeared to be swallowing him up like fuzzy blue water about to drown him. Phillip had always been so big and strong. Now it looked like the yellow balloon he held could pick him up and float him away. Phillip watched her silent reaction to see if she understood what he was telling her.

"It means I'm going to go away, Pen. And I won't be able to come back."

Penelope's panic grew. Why was Phillip saying all of these horrible things? Suddenly she wanted to leave the balcony, to run away, to run from the panic that ate at her throat and the sobs rising in her chest. Most of all, she wanted to run away from Phillip, away from his skinny hands and sunken cheeks, away from his bald head and his wheelchair, and most of all away from his words. But she knew she couldn't run away, because how could she leave Phillip, Phillip who had taught her to swim, Phillip who made her laugh, Phillip who always treated her like she was as smart as everybody else? She swallowed her fear enough to speak.

"Are you going up in the sky, Phillip? Like they say in church . . . are you going up to heaven?" Phillip nodded his head. Penelope wrapped her short fingers around his hand, and they sat silently for a moment holding on to one another. Then Phillip gathered his courage to speak again.

"But Penelope, after I'm gone, I'll need you to do something for me." Phillip had Penelope's attention once more. Sure that she was listening closely, he continued. "Just because I'm up in heaven, doesn't mean you can't talk to me anymore." Penelope looked at her brother, confused and hopeful at the same time. He pointed at the balloon. "Whenever you want to talk to me, I want you to write down everything you want to say on a note and tie it to the end of a balloon. Then you can let go of the balloon, and it will bring your message up to me in heaven." Phillip's voice cracked, and he swallowed. "Can you do that for me, Pen?"

Penelope slowly nodded her head as tears rolled down her cheeks. She stared intently into her brother's face. She had never seen Phillip cry, but tears were rolling from his eyes as well. Penelope wished for all the world that she could make Phillip stay, that she could make time stop forever and they could sit on this balcony always, just the two of them hand in hand. But all she could do was take a deep breath. "Yes, Phillip," she promised.

Then Phillip's fingers relaxed, the string gently slipped from his grasp, and brother and sister watched as the yellow balloon floated silently into the sky.

UNDERSTANDING DEATH

Most children learn about death when they are young. Death is a very difficult thing to understand, and most people learn about it in stages. Often our first experience of death is when a pet or a relative dies. Over the years, we come to understand that death is a part of life and something that everyone must eventually face.

It is very common for people with mental retardation to learn about death later than other people do or to have more trouble understanding death than other people have. Penelope's parents try to shield her from death. Even when it is plain that Phillip is dying, they do not tell Penelope what is going on. This is a common reaction among family members and friends of people with intellectual disabilities. They want to protect the person from the pain, sorrow, and confusion that death causes. This, however, is usually not a good way to deal with the subject of death, because even though it is painful and we would often like to ignore its existence, we can't stop death from happening. As much as we would like to, we can't always shield people from pain. Think how much more painful it would be if no one prepared Penelope for Phillip's death. Then when he did die, she would not have expected it and wouldn't have had a chance to say good-bye.

Just because all people must eventually learn about death, however, doesn't mean it will be easy to understand. A person with mental retardation may think that someone who has died has simply gone away temporarily and will be coming back or has gone to sleep and will wake up. Many organizations offer special classes for people with mental retardation to teach them about death and to help them deal with the painful emotions that death might cause. You can learn about such classes and other services by looking on

Death is a difficult concept for everyone.

To a person with mental retardation, death may seem like a dark world into which they can only peek.

the Internet, asking a local hospital, or by doing research at a library.

Learning about death can be frightening for people with mental retardation for another reason. Most people with mental retardation will need extra help and care through their whole lives. Penelope, for example, is twenty-one but still lives with her mother and father. It is not unusual for young people this age to still be living with their parents, but a person with mental retardation will often continue living at home where he can get the care and support he needs throughout his adulthood. However, many families of people with mental retardation live with the fear of not

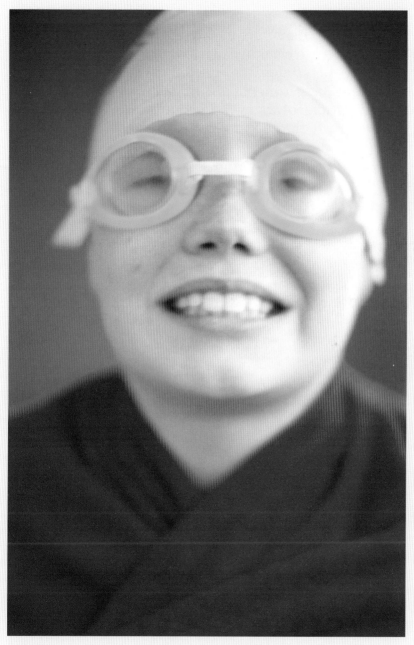

Penelope's swimming skills are an important and enduring gift given to her by her brother.

knowing what will happen to their children when they die. Parents usually die before their children do, and when this happens, people with mental retardation may be left without the support system they need. Just like Penelope's parents, many parents do not discuss death with their mentally retarded children. Lack of knowledge, however, can create huge amounts of anxiety for both the parents and the child.

Parents will not always be around to teach their children, but most children will grow up and no longer need their parents as much. Parents of a child with mental retardation must make plans for the future, when they may no longer be around to help their child.

Parents should make plans for how their children will be cared for after the parents pass away. More importantly, in most cases, parents should discuss these plans with their child so that the child can feel empowered by having knowledge instead of frightened by being left with uncertainty.

New strengths are born from change.
—Lucie Stone

8

MESSAGES TO HEAVEN

Penelope sat at her new kitchen table composing a letter to Phillip.

"Dear Phillip." Penelope carefully printed the words in large, block letters, her tongue sticking out as she wrote. "Today is the bestest day!" She brushed a long lock of hair out of her eye and concentrated even harder. "Sara is moving in today. Our new apartment is grate!" Penelope looked around her tiny apartment and felt a keen sense of pride. "I luv working at the bakry and my apartment smells grate all the time!"

Penelope had gotten a job working at the bakery below her apartment. Sometimes she put the fresh loaves of bread out into their baskets, and sometimes she worked at the cash register carefully typing the numbers into the machine and hitting the button to add them all up. Penelope loved working at the bakery, and she loved the bakery's owner Mrs. Harold. In fact, it was Mrs. Harold's idea to let Penelope and her best friend Sara move into the apartment above the little bread shop. The apartment always smelled like fresh bread, and Penelope was only a flight of stairs away from work.

As Penelope finished composing her letter, the buzzer rang. She ran to the front door and hit the button on the intercom. "Who is it?" Penelope spoke in a businesslike tone. Using the intercom made her feel adult and important.

"It's Ss-s-Sara." A happy voice crackled up through the speaker. Penelope clapped her hands.

"Okay, you can come up." She pressed the other button to unlock the door downstairs and soon heard Sara's footsteps in the hall. Penelope opened the door to see her friend's smiling face. Sara's mother trudged a few feet behind, a giant box in hand.

"Where should I put my ss-s-stuff?" Sara asked. Penelope ushered her friend into the apartment. "My mom came tt-t-to help." Sara pointed over her shoulder and made a funny face. Penelope giggled behind her hand.

"Are you girls laughing at me?" Sara's mother spoke with fake sternness, and Sara and Penelope shook their heads in denial.

Penelope waved her arm, beckoning Sara and her mother to follow, and led the two women into Sara's bedroom. At first, Penelope had wanted to share a bedroom with Sara, but Sara wanted her own bedroom. She had a boyfriend and sometimes she would be coming in late—and she wanted a place where she could be alone with her boyfriend. That was okay with Penelope. She respected Sara's desire for privacy and knew that they would still have a lot of fun, even if they weren't sharing a room.

Penelope also knew that living in her own apartment wasn't all about having fun. It was also about responsibility. She would have to do her own laundry and cook food and pay bills. Living by herself would be hard work! But she and Sara were going to help each other. And Penelope knew that her mom, dad, Krista, and Jonathan would be stopping by almost every day whether she wanted them to or not.

So many things had changed in Penelope's life. When her brother Phillip died, an empty hole had been left in her heart. She thought she would never be happy again. And she couldn't talk to her mom or dad about how she felt because they were so sad, too. Penelope was afraid that if she talked about Phillip, it would make them even sadder. Krista and Jonathan tried to do things to make her happy, but it just wasn't the same. They couldn't make her laugh the way Phillip could, and they couldn't make her forget that Phillip was gone.

Talking to Sara had helped Penelope start to feel better. Sara knew what it felt like to be sad. Sara used to feel sad when her stepbrother did bad things to her. Later, when she finally told her mother, her mother made Sara's stepbrother move out. But Sara hadn't felt happy right away. It took a long time for her to feel happy again. When Penelope talked to Sara about her own sadness, Sara didn't try to make her laugh or forget about Phillip. Instead, Sara said, "It's okay, Penelope. Ss-s-sometimes you just have tt-o be ss-sad." Lot's of people thought Sara was stupid because she stuttered, but when she said things like that, Penelope thought Sara was very smart.

So with Sara's permission and support, Penelope felt sad about Phillip for a long time. But then she started writing letters to him, just the way he had told her. She tied the letters to the end of balloons, and then let the balloons float away to carry her messages to heaven.

In her messages, Penelope told Phillip all kinds of things. She told Phillip about how sad she was that he was gone and how much she missed him. She told him about how sometimes she would dream about him, and in her dreams he'd be swimming fast like a fish and looking all strong and healthy the way he did before the sickness in his brain. She told him about how she and Sara were still such good friends and that bad things had happened to Sara, but she had learned to be happy again anyway. She told him about how Krista and her husband had a baby; his name was Phillip, too, and how Jonathan's paintings had been in a show where they won lots of prizes, just like the prizes Penelope won at Special Olympics. Penelope told Phillip about how she still went to Special Olympics, but now she was a coach, helping kids who were just like her when she was little.

Day after day, as Penelope wrote, she began to feel better. It happened so slowly that she didn't even realize at first that something was changing. But then one day as she watched a yellow balloon float away into the sky, she realized that she wasn't crying the way she normally did when she sent letters to Phillip. Instead, she was looking into the sunny sky, watching the yellow balloon disappear, and smiling.

It was that very same day that she saw the "Help Wanted" sign in the bakery window and ran home to tell her parents that she wanted a job. Penelope was very nervous when she told them because she thought they might say no. They had looked at each other with questioning expressions. Then they both smiled and said they thought it was a great idea. After that, all kinds of things changed. Now Penelope had a job, money of her own, and even an apartment where she got to live with her best friend.

"Can you help us carry more things from the car?" Sara's mother broke into Penelope's thoughts.

"Yes, I just have to do something." Penelope rushed back to the kitchen table. She picked up the pencil and began to write again.

"I have to go now," she printed in her wavy letters. "I will rite more later." Then after a moment she added, "I am realy happy today. Love, Penelope."

Penelope tied the letter to the string of a yellow balloon and carried it to the open window. She opened her hand and watched as her message disappeared into the sky.

CAN PEOPLE WITH MENTAL RETARDATION LIVE ON THEIR OWN?

Many people with mental retardation will continue living with family members for their whole lives. But many others get apartments and houses of their own. They still might need help sometimes with things like money, paying bills, grocery shopping, or cleaning, but many people with mental retardation are quite capable of living on their own.

Some people with mental retardation may choose to live in assisted living communities—housing just for people with disabilities where there are staff members to help them if they have any problems. Other people may have roommates or spouses who can help them. Still other people will be able to live in their own apartments or houses, just like anybody else.

CAN PEOPLE WITH MENTAL RETARDATION HAVE JOBS?

In the past, many people thought that individuals with mental retardation were helpless, had nothing to contribute, and couldn't hold jobs. Today we realize that this is not true at all. While schools and agencies for people with mental retardation once concentrated on academic abilities, today there is a growing focus on social and interpersonal abilities instead. Intelligence tests play a decreasing role in assessing the strengths of these individuals, while professionals look now toward using the strengths of the individual, community, and family to improve the quality of life for those who have this disability. Vocational training plays a bigger part in the educational plan than it once did, and more and more schools are developing links with businesses and industries, so that many children with mental retardation will one day be able to be self-supporting.

Our society used to see treatment for mentally retarded individuals as "charity." Today we think more in terms of "rights." In 1971, the United Nations' Declaration on the Rights of Mentally Retarded Individuals stated that these people have the right to "medical care, physical therapy, and the education, training, rehabilitation, and guidance needed to develop the individual's potential." U.S. courts now look to this U.N. declaration as they include individuals with mental retardation under the Constitution's protection of individual rights. Once people like Penelope were neglected, abused, and denied life-saving medical treatment. Today mentally retarded individuals have their own self-advocacy group.

Just like everybody else, individuals with intellectual disabilities have both strengths and weaknesses. By finding

A child with mental retardation enjoys learning to swim at Camp Abilities in New York State.

Rock climbing offers children with mental retardation a chance to experience the excitement of success.

and developing one's skills and talents, many people can find jobs that they are both good at and enjoy. Some companies now even go out of their way to hire people with mental disabilities. In certain cases, these companies have found that people with mental disabilities work so hard to succeed that they are actually harder working and more conscientious than other employees.

Some people with mental retardation work in regular jobs. Others may not have the skills or training to do these jobs or may not be able to work in the stressful atmosphere of the average workplace. However, there are still other employment options. Many people with mental disabilities work in places called sheltered workshops. These are places that only employ people with disabilities. Sheltered workshops give people a place where they can work in a safe

Exercise builds both physical fitness and self-esteem in young people with mental retardation.

and lower-stress atmosphere. Many people also like working in sheltered workshops because it gives them an opportunity to socialize with friends.

Employment is a very important part of adult life. It is one of the ways that individuals find a sense of purpose, accomplishment, confidence, and satisfaction. Through employment, we achieve and communicate our adult **status** in society. For many people with mental retardation, employment is a way to gain independence and adulthood in a world that insists on treating them like children.

DEALING WITH PAINFUL EMOTIONS

At first, Penelope does not know how to deal with her emotions when her brother dies. Having a friend helps her. Sara has dealt with many painful emotions in her own life, so she is able to give Penelope the support and understanding that she needs.

Phillip himself also gave Penelope a powerful tool for dealing with his death. When he taught Penelope to tie letters to balloons to "carry her messages to heaven," he gave Penelope a way to still have a relationship with him even after he was gone. Whether a person has mental retardation or not, she still needs to learn to cope with loss. Finding a way to remain connected to the people that we love, even when they die, is an important step in coming to terms with death. As Penelope learns to accept the death of her brother, she also learns how to continue living a full and happy life.

FURTHER READING

Bowman-Kruhm, Mary. *Everything You Need to Know About Down Syndrome*. New York: Rosen, 2000.

Castles, Elaine E. *"We're People First": The Social and Emotional Lives of Individuals with Mental Retardation*. Westport, Conn.: Praeger, 1996.

Esherick, Joan. *Journey Toward Recovery: Youth With Brain Injury*. Philadelphia: Mason Crest Publishers, 2004.

Kaufman, Sandra Z. *Retarded Isn't Stupid, Mom!* Baltimore, Md.: Paul H. Brookes, 1999.

Penley, Gary. *Della Raye: A Girl Who Grew Up in Hell and Emerged Whole*. Gretna, La.: Pelican, 2000.

Simon, Rachel. *Riding the Bus with My Sister: A True Life Journey*. Boston: Houghton Mifflin, 2002.

Trainer, Marilyn and Helen Featherstone. *Differences in Common: Straight Talk On Mental Retardation, Down Syndrome, and Your Life*. Bethesda, Md.: Woodbine House, 2003.

Zuckoff, Mitchell. *Choosing Naia: A Family's Journey*. Boston: Beacon Press, 2002.

FOR MORE INFORMATION

The ARC of the United States
www.thearc.org

The Center for an Accessible Society
www.accessiblesociety.org

Inclusion International
www.inclusion-international.org

LDOnline (Information about learning disorders)
www.ldonline.org

Mainstream Online (News and advocacy in disability rights)
www.mainstream-mag.com

National Association for Down Syndrome
www.nads.org

National Down Syndrome Society
www.ndss.org

The National Fragile X Foundation
www.fragilex.org

Special Olympics
www.specialolympics.org

Publisher's Note:

The Web sites listed on this page were active at the time of publication.
The publisher is not responsible for Web sites that have changed their ad-
dress or discontinued operation since the date of publication. The publisher will review and update the Web sites upon each reprint.

GLOSSARY

access: The right to enter, have, or make use of something.

activists: People who work to promote a specific cause.

amniocentesis: A medical procedure in which a needle is inserted through a pregnant woman's abdomen and into her uterus to take a sample of the fluid that surrounds the growing baby. Tests are performed on the cells in the fluid to learn about the baby's health.

apnea: A condition where a person (often a baby) stops breathing for short periods of time.

civil rights: The basic rights that citizens of a country are guaranteed to have such as the right to free speech and the right to freedom from discrimination.

cognitive: Relating to mental processes such as thought, awareness, reasoning, perception, and judgment.

developmental: Relating to growth or development.

discrimination: Prejudice or unfair treatment.

DNA: The molecules within each living cell that contain the genetic codes which dictate the characteristics of that organism.

epilepsy: A term given to conditions in which a person's brain gives off irregular and uncontrolled electrical impulses resulting in seizures (altered consciousness and/or jerking contractions and relaxations of the body's muscles).

eugenics: The study or practice of preventing certain people from having children while allowing others to do so for the purpose of improving human genetics.

familial: Relating to a family.

fetus: In humans, the unborn child from the end of the eighth week after conception until birth.

genetic: Of or relating to the information carried in the genes.

group homes: Homes where groups of people with disabilities are provided shelter and care. In many cases, these have replaced the large institutions that once cared for people with mental retardation. Group homes allow people with disabilities to receive the supervision they need while still being a part of the community.

Holocaust: The name given to Hitler's and the Nazi Party's 1940's campaign to kill all of the Jewish people, Gypsies, and other people they found "undesirable."

hypertension: High blood pressure.

hypothyroidism: When the thyroid is underproductive.

incubator: An apparatus with a chamber that provides a warm and nurturing environment for premature or sick babies.

infringe: To violate or trespass upon.

neurological: Having to do with the nervous system—the brain, the spinal cord, and the nerves.

oral communication: Spoken communication, communication through a person's voice.

peers: People of the same age group.

phenylketonuria: An inherited disease that causes the individual to be unable to metabolize phenylalanine, an amino acid; untreated, phenylketonuria causes severe mental retardation.

placenta previa: A condition where the placenta (the organ that connects a fetus to the mother's uterus) is placed over the cervix (the opening from the uterus into the vagina). It can cause dangerous blood loss for the mother, and it can also retard the baby's growth or make the baby grow abnormally.

quotient: An amount or measurement.

social skills: The skills and abilities that allow one to interact successfully with other people.

solidarity: Fellowship, a union of interests, purposes, or sympathies.

status: Place in society, a measure of worth, wealth, or prestige.

sterilized: Performed a medical procedure to prevent a person from ever having children.

stigmatized: Branded as disgraceful, worthless, or something to be looked down upon.

symmetry: Where two halves of something are mirror images of one another. Normally, the human face is fairly symmetrical—the right eye matches the left eye, the right side of the mouth is the same shape as the left side of the mouth, etc.—but some kinds of mental retardation can cause a person's face to appear "lopsided," lacking symmetry.

thyroid: A gland in the neck responsible for producing hormones (chemicals that affect the body's growth and functioning).

toxemia: An abnormal condition that can occur during pregnancy where the kidneys fail to filter out toxic substances, allowing them to pass into the mother's bloodstream.

traumatic: Causing serious physical or emotional injury.

INDEX

BIOGRAPHIES

Joyce Libal is a writer and artist living with her husband and assorted pets on their orchard in the mountains of northeastern Pennsylvania. When she is not writing, Joyce enjoys painting, quilting, and gardening. She has written several books for other Mason Crest series, including PSYCHIATRIC DISORDERS: DRUGS AND PSYCHOLOGY FOR THE MIND AND BODY AND CAREERS WITH CHARACTER.

Dr. Lisa Albers is a developmental behavioral pediatrician at Children's Hospital Boston and Harvard Medical School, where her responsibilities include outpatient pediatric teaching and patient care in the Developmental Medicine Center. She currently is Director of the Adoption Program, Director of Fellowships in Developmental and Behavioral Pediatrics, and collaborates in a consultation program for community health centers. She is also the school consultant for the Walker School, a residential school for children in the state foster care system.

Dr. Carolyn Bridgemohan is an instructor in pediatrics at Harvard Medical School and is a board-certified developmental behavioral pediatrician on staff in the Developmental Medicine Center at Children's Hospital, Boston. Her clinical practice includes children and youth with autism, hearing impairment, developmental language disorders, global delays, mental retardation, and attention and learning disorders. Dr. Bridgemohan is coeditor of *Bright Futures Case Studies for Primary Care Clinicians: Child Development and Behavior*, a curriculum used nationwide in pediatric residency training programs.

Cindy Croft is the State Special Needs Director in Minnesota, coordinating Project EXCEPTIONAL MN, through Concordia University. Project EXCEPTIONAL MN is a state project that supports the inclusion of children in community settings through training, on-site consultation, and professional development. She also teaches as adjunct faculty for Concordia University, St. Paul, Minnesota. She has worked in the special needs arena for the past fifteen years.

Dr. Laurie Glader is a developmental pediatrician at Children's Hospital in Boston where she directs the Cerebral Palsy Program and is a staff pediatrician with the Coordinated Care Services, a program designed to meet the needs of children with special health care needs. Dr. Glader also teaches regularly at Harvard Medical School. Her work with public agencies includes New England SERVE, an organization that builds connections between state health departments, health care organizations, community providers, and families. She is also the staff physician at the Cotting School, a school specializing in the education of children with a wide range of special health care needs.